DECEMBER 2022

AN ANTHOLOGY OF ARTICLES

BRAIN BOOSTER ARTICLES

Made with ❤ on the Notion Press Platform
www.notionpress.com

Contents

Preface v

1. Farmer's Suicide In India : Challenges & Viable Policy Options 1

2. A Study On E-governance Will Reduce The Workburn Of The Government Worker 11

3. Sampling,replay/interpolation,mashups In The Music And Entertainment Law 23

4. Convention On The Elimination Of All Forms Of Discrimination Against Women 29

5. De Facto Marriage:live- In- Relations: Unmarried Couples: Rights And Obligations 36

6. Personality Rights: Significance And Role In Present World 39

7. Female Genital Mutilation 45

8. Public Opinion On Increasing School Dropout 49

9. An Analysis On The Evolution Of Surrogacy Bills With Special Reference To 2019 And 2020 Bill 66

10. The Psychology Of Judicial Sentencing 74

11. Practicalities Associated With Admissibility Of Electronic Evidence 78

Preface

"Start writing, no matter what. The water does not flow until the faucet is turned on".

• Louis L'Amour

This book is a bouquet of articles contributed by students, professors and academicians. Hundreds of students and professors are contributing their work to Brain Booster Articles, we are here to provide ample information about Law and Contemporary issues. Our aim is to provide a platform for today's generation to express their views and ideas on law and contemporary law.

FARMER'S SUICIDE IN INDIA : CHALLENGES & VIABLE POLICY OPTIONS

Author: Sanjoli Verma, V year of B.A.,LL.B. from Hidayatullah National Law University

Hypothesis

This project focuses mainly on the effects of growing suicides of farmers in India. Because of inflation, liberalisation and privatisation in India, the living standards of farmers in India are threatened. The effects of the open market and subsequent competitiveness and pressure have led farmers to severe debt which leads to suicides. According to reports by the National Crime Records Office, the suicide rate of farmers in India has not improved considerably.The purpose of this study is to explore & investigate the challenges and solutions to reduce farm suicides in India.

Research Limitations

The study recognises that while many factors play a role in raising the suicide of farmers in India, it is only possible that many variables are needed. This suggests that the increase in farmers' suicide has many causes that could lead to this problem in the country and that this research does not have to carry out a further qualitative study in depth. Hence all of the factors may not be directly involved in any one particular area as different regions possess different issues which lead to such drastic steps by farmers. Still it is difficult to formulate a policy which can be applicable and compatible for framers for allover India. Moreover economic & social betterment is something which is difficult to reach for each and every farmer. Their exploitation should be averted as large as possible.

Introduction

India is an agricultural country that relies directly or indirectly on agriculture, for about 70 percent of its population. But the suicides of farmers in India are worrisome. According to the Central Government, over 12000 suicides have been registered each year since 2013, despite a multi-pronged approach to improving farmers' income and social security. Around 10 percent of all suicides occur in India in farmers' suicides.

The threat of farmers' suicides cannot be denied and goes against the ambitions of the demographic dividend to reap benefits. The aim and the way forward is to discuss the suicides of farmers in India in this article.The word 'suicide' suggests voluntary killing yourself. In a study by Patel et al., suicide in India has been shown to be a completely different epidemic from the high income countries (HICs). There are a number of suicides in India each year. The number of suicides is nearly double in rural areas, although there is no variation in HICs.

The statistics in India reveal a steady rise in suicide levels, with Maharashtra, MP, Telangana, Andhra Paresh, Tamil Nadu,Chhattisgarh and Karnataka being the countries with the highest number of suicides. These states together accounted for approximately 90% of the overall suicides of farmers in India.

The list consists of farmers-growers and farmers. Self-harming was committed both by marginal farmers and small farmers. The worst affected state is Maharashtra. Ironically, the most beneficial part of Punjab from the Green Revolution also has a depressing image of Indian farmers' suicides. Between 1995 and 2015 there were 4,687 farmers suicides, of which 1334 from one Mansa district alone, in the state of Punjab.

Causes and Reasons for these Suicides

The problem of farmer suicides has assumed a serious proportion. According to the National Crime Record Bureau (NCRB), 10%of the total suicide rates in India are suicides by farmers.Among the causes of farmers' suicides in India, scholars have provided different explanations, such as mozon failure, climate change, high debt burdens, public policies, mental health, personal problems and family issues.

The surge in the cost of input: The growing pressure on farmers due to the high price of agricultural inputs was one of the major causes of farmers' suicides in India. These factors culminate in the overall cost rise for wheat, which currently is three times the price in 2005.

Cost of chemicals and seeds: whether fertilisers, crop protection chemicals or seeds for planting, for already indebted farmers, agriculture has become costly.

Costs of farming equipment: However, production costs are not limited to the fundamental raw materials. The already high costs are added by the use of farm equipment and machines, such as tractors, submersible pumps etc. Furthermore, for the small and marginal farmers these secondary inputs have become less accessible.

Costs of labour: In the same way, it becomes more expensive to employ staff and livestock. Although it may represent an improvement in workers' socio-economic status, which is primarily driven by MGNERGA and a rise in basic minimum revenues, the boost in the agriculture industry has not been too successful.

Distressed due to loans

NCRB data indicates the victims had unpaid loans from local banks in 2474 of the 3,000 farmer suicides studied in 2015. An indication of the links between the two is plain enough. However, it is a lengthy debate that includes more clear empirical proof whether or not the banks were bullying them.

In addition, it was evident from the normal trend that only 9,8 percent of the loans borrowed by these farmers were borrowed from the money lenders. Those who give money will not be able, as otherwise considered, to exert leverage or muscle power as a driving force

The proliferation of both reflects another clear connection between suicides and debt by farmers. Though 1293 indebtedness suicides were committed by Maharashtra, Karnataka did have 946. Notice that both countries have seen one of the highest suicide and debt incidences in farmers.

Lack of Direct Market Integration: While initiatives like the Contract Farming help to integrate the producers directly into the market, there is a reduction in the position of the intermediaries.

Lack of Knowledge: the digital dividity and the literature gap have put small and marginal farmers, because they have been unable to use the positive aspects of government policies, particularly vulnerable. This is expressed in ongoing unsustainable crops – such as growing sugar cane in regions with water deficits.

Water crisis: The concentration of these suicides in regions with water deficits like Karnataka and Maharashtra is an indication that the water crisis and thus inability to meet the demand for output have exacerbated the danger. This is particularly true in the context of continuing failed monsoons.

Inter-state water conflicts & disputes : the fact that each other's water needs among the states were not met adds to the already prevailing crisis. A recent Kaveri controversy, in which Karnataka and Tamil Nadu fought both in and outside the tribunal to overcome water shortage even in so far as the court award is not complied with, is at issue.

Climatic Change: As the last nail in the coffin, climate change has led to more uncertainties associated with the already unpredictable monsoon mechanism and thus agricultural activity. Delayed monsoons experienced shortfall in production year after year, while incidents such as flash flutter resulted in crop losses.

New Economic policies led by urban consumption in India: India's political economy is more powered than rural producers by urban consumers.This is expressed in the importance of price checks when prices escalate and a failed withdrawal once the price is regulated (imposed minimum export prices, the entry of goods under the Critical Commodities etc.). In contrast, we imposed a minimum import price to ensure our steel industry. This unequal treatment of the primary sector often reduces the profit margin and thus prevents farmers from breaking off the debt cycle.The root cause of farmers' suicides is structural shifts in Indian government macro-economic policy which favour privatisation, liberalisation, and globalisation.

Loan waivers rather restructing & re-investing measures: We have adopted a policy of appeasement as the latest decision by the UP government to withdraw Rs 36,000 pounds of loans. The government has taken a policy of managing agricultural indebtedness. Surprisingly, at a time when farm yields in the aftermath of an excellent monsoon are predicted to be higher.

Essentially, the reasons are crop failure, non-sustainable production and subsequent agricultural debt, which contributes to the failure to reinforce the farmers' economic status as driving forces behind the suicides.

Challenges - Issues with current policy

In 1991, the Indian economy's liberalising policies led to a "agrarian crisis" and increased suicides of farmers. The government's policy led to market opening was the principal cause of 'agrarian crises.' The number of policies that the government has implemented are thought to be beneficial to agriculture, and it certainly has changed the face of Indian farming, but this has led to a growing death rate amongst farmers. The 1991 strategy led to improvements in aggregate and public investment institutions.

The changes brought on by Government policy of 1991 raised input costs while output rates have declined or become even more volatile. The price of inputs has increased. These changes have especially badly hit producers of small and marginal landowners who grow cash crops, such as coffee and cotton. All India's Vijoo Krishnan Kisan Sabha blames high input and decreased output costs of cultivation. Many farmers produce each year at a loss. The bad irrigation facilities and reduced subsidies cause farming to be risky every day are the main reasons for the rising number of suicides.

Different Responses & Policies to Suicides of the Farmers

Here are some of the key aid packages and the government's debt waiver schemes:

2006 relief package — targeted mainly at 31 districts with high relative incidences of farmers' suicides in four countries of Andhra Pradesh, Maharashtra, Karnataka and the Kerala. In order to alleviate these farmers' suffering, a special rehabilitation programme was initiated. The package provided farmers with debt relief, a strengthened institutional credit supply, enhanced irrigation services, experts and social workers for agricultural support and implemented subsidiary income opportunities through horticulture, livestock, dairy and fishing. The Government of India has also revealed the Prime Minister's National Relief Fund to farmers for its ex-gratia cash assistance.

Agricultural debt waiver and debt relief scheme, 2008 – over 36 million farmers were benefiting from the Agricultural Debt Waiver and Debt Relief Scheme, which cost 65,000 rupees (USD 10 billion). This expenditure was intended to write down both the interest due by the farmers and the portion of the loan principal.

2013 Income diversification programme – the Indian Government has initiated a Special Livestock and Fishery Package for the Andhra Pradesh, Maharashtra, Karnataka and Kerala suicide-prone farming regions in 2013. The goal of the package was to diversify farmers' income streams.

In addition to these Central Government initiatives the state governments such as Maharashtra Bill, in 2008, and the Kerala Farmers' Debt Relief Commission (amendment) Bill, 2012 are making great effort to control the conditions for farming loans.

The government even tries to conduct of national and state-wise farmers' suicides (Statistics) and surveys.

Regional surveys : Several Indian government agencies have conducted their own attempts to discourage suicides of farmers. The Maharashtra Government formed a special group in 2006, known as the Amravati-based Vasantrao Naik ShetiSwavlamban Mission, to address agricultural distress. Also, under the Chairmanship of Dr. Veeresh, former Vice Chancellor of the Agricultural University and Professor Deshpande, the Government of Karnataka was formed as a group to research farmer suicides.

2010 Maharashtra Relief Package : The Maharashtra State Government made it illegal to pursue repayment of loans for non-licensed creditors in 2010. The state government also announced that it would provide government loans, the low-rate crop insurance programme whose premium will be charged 50% by farmers and 50% by government, the launching of alternative income opportunities for farmers in high suicide prone regions, including poultry, milk products and sericulture.

<u>New policies formulated regarding this issue</u>

In 2004, under the leadership of Dr. M.S. Swaminathan, the government created the National Farmers Commission. The Commission's main objective was to develop methods for increasing the profitability, efficiency and sustainability of the major agricultural sector. The "National Farmers Policy 2007" has been formulated and accepted by the Government of India, following the recommendations made by the Commission.

The aims of that policy are, among other things, to improve the economical viability of farms and to provide adequate price policy, risk management measures and significantly improve farmers' net income in addition to improvements in production, profitability, property, water and support.

On international standards UNCSD is urging the international farmers community to consider and deal with the rising issue of suicide.

<u>**Effectiveness of such Government Responses**</u>

Even though many measures were taken by the government but many policies responses and reliefs packages of the government were largely unsuccessful, misdirected, inefficient and deficient states. In addition to jobs, productive activities and agricultural prosperity, it focuses on credit and loan. Assistance in paying unpaid assets and benefits helps the lenders, but it has not succeeded in creating stable and good income sources for the farmers. The usurious money lenders keep borrowing at the rate between 24 and 50%, while the land the farmer is working on remains poor in income generating capacity, subject to conditions of the weather.

The government has been unable to understand that debt relief only deferred the problem and that only stable sources of revenue, increased crop yields per hectare, irrigation and other infrastructure safety can provide a longer-term solution to the distress of farms. Golait recognised the positive position of the Crop diversification initiative in government response to farmers' suicide reports in a Reserve Bank of India paper.

Indian agriculture is still suffering: (i) low productivity; (ii) falling water levels; (iii) high loans; (iv) a distorted market; (iii) many middlemen and intermediaries who raise costs but not add a high value to them; (ii) legislation stifling private investment; (iii) controlled prices; (iii). The method therefore does not benefit agriculture with the mere focus on credit isolated from the above factors. In addition, a more pro-active position in developing and sustaining reliable irrigation and other agricultural infrastructure is required to resolve the distress of farmers in India.

<u>**Recommendation, Measures and Suggestions**</u>

1. The growing concern about suicide farmers has forced Mr Dvendra Fadnavis to launch an integrated scheme to guarantee small and marginal farmers economic sustainability. "There have been 25 lakh farmers in the value chain of all the main crops agreed by the State." Mr Fadnavis will work along with 40 companies that have ensured investment in the Maharashtra

agriculture sectors.

2. At the same time, a new holistic strategy focusing on government-private-sector investor partnerships and improved irrigation potentials is also being implemented to improve the livelihoods of farmers.

3. In order to minimise agriculture's reliance on money lenders, the farmers' daily income must be taken into account.

4. There was a need to implement alternative livelihoods such as journals etc., and the government started to work on these schemes to ensure farmers' survival even in the event of agricultural failures.

5. Integrated prevention of harmful pest control policies – To avoid crop damage, an all-inclusive approach should be applied that incorporates ecological, chemical, mechanical and physical methodology. In that case it might be a good way to get motivated by the early Vietnamese rule of no-spray (predatory beets for biological pest control are preserved, the criterion of cutting pesticide by 50 percent).

6. Reducing fertiliser costs – The input costs can be reduced by helping fertiliser industries reduce costs through internal funding rather than external borrowing.

7. Leverage scientific and technological developments by making sure the state-owned seed policy focuses on new genotypes, contract farming and weather sensitization.

8. Precision farming techniques such as SRI must be promoted (Systematic Rice Intensification).

9. In order to ensure cheaper local production, the policy and subsidies on farm equipment should concentrate on the imported equipment and try out some motivation such as duty credit scripts. Subsidies have to be redistributed to capital generation and business custom hire centres (CHCs) and implemented promptly.

10. Corporate social responsibility (CSR), particularly in the area of capacity-building, skill development and the development of CHCs, must be encouraged in the agricultural sector.

11. Institutional funding should also be assured that the elite within the agricultural community are sufficient and inclusive rather than catering for.

12. Cooperative farming between small and marginalised farmers must be encouraged to ensure that they are not laid waste while the big farmers profit at their expense.

13. It is a healthy goal to double farmers' income by 2022, but credit waivers cannot be a response. Sustainable, reinvestment- and restructuring-

providing agriculture instead is the way ahead. The position of the State is one of liberation, but empowerment is what the primary sector and the farmer requires.

14. Directive interventions:

• early warning signals for unsustainable lending, which would enable both the burdened farmers and stressed banks to take a two-pronged approach.

• Wherever practicable, options for restructuring credits must be included.

• Claims for insurance must be settled promptly and fairly.

• A District wise list of indebted farmers should be considered as well as efforts to de-stress them by means of advices and alternatives. The situation must be monitored and increased by NABARD and local administrations to reduce farmers' suicide.

15. The engagement of civil society organisations will employ creative efforts such as crowd-funding (CSOs). Efforts such as zoning for agro-climatic goods, DD Kisan education, Soil Health Card scheme for agriculture, various insurance policies for crops, etc.

16. Community consciousness needs to be developed through the use of a role model approach which highlights progress made by farmers benefitting from sustainable and climate-friendly farming practises.

17. Use of technology: new technologies are required to increase production per unit of soil and water.

18. National Agricultural Biosafety System: the biosafety system to be developed to coordinate the agricultural bioprogramme.

19. Credit & Insurance: Development of credit counselling centres to support seriously debt-rescuing farmers to get away from the debt trap. Gyan Chaupals needs to assist in the challenge for both credit and insurance literacy in villages.

20. Minimum Price of support (MSP) mechanisms to be efficiently enforced in the country in order to guarantee remuneration rates for farm products.

Covid -19 and Suicide of Farmers

Concerning COVID 19, individuals and communities face psychosocial problems that can be special and severe in marginalised populations, such as Indian farmers who already have an ongoing psychosocial burden of suicidal behaviour. Apart from normal mental health operations, the social determinants of suicide behaviour, including social and economic support, should be assessed in this population and multi-pronounced, multi-level approaches should be taken. In addition, it is crucial to acknowledge and resolve suicide among vulnerable farmers in India through well-considered policy work between mental health practitioners, academics, health policymakers and stakeholders from social welfare authorities.

Conclusion

We must be very careful & keep a close watch and try to curb root causes which leads farmers' to such extents. Since farmers' suicides are a matter of serious concern for a rapidly developed country and a problem for well-planned financial infrastructure, village officials such as local Revenue owe their responsibility for this action. The duty of investigating the financial wellbeing of all farmers should be delegated to them. They are not only responsible for inquiries; they are also responsible for advising distressed farmers and helping them through bank litigation in the case that they are trapped in any debt.

Changes in market reforms are also needed to ensure that agreements between farmers and buyers are equitable. Certain adjustments must be made in the strategies and policies of the government. It is best to take proactive steps to contain this situation, instead of spending later on the relief package to deal with the suicides of farmers. On both social and economic fronts preventive steps should be tackled. In this regard there should be no over-emphasising the importance of financial literacy, education, advice and medical services for social purposes.

CHAPTER TWO

A STUDY ON E-GOVERNANCE WILL REDUCE THE WORKBURN OF THE GOVERNMENT WORKER

Author: L. Natanio Selladurai, V year of B.A.,LL.B.(Hons.) from Saveetha School of Law

ABSTRACT

This paper studies one governance will reduce the work burn of the government workers.The reason to consist of e-governance to government is to method extra efficiently in numerous components. Whether it means to lessen price with the aid of lowering paper clutter, staffing price, or communicating with private citizens or public government.The application of e-trade for more efficient government transactions sports.this paper analyses that e governance will reduce the work burn of government workers,to study about an e governance.This study is based on both doctrinal and empirical method.the data for empirical method was created by understanding a survey. It is based on primary data and secondary information.The primary data for the study was collected from sample 200 respondents,The study used a survey questionnaire to collect the data and we used percentage analysis for a meaningful analysis.Very essential element in the entire system of Governance is the overall performance of personnel, which ends up in fulfillment of goals. Nowadays lot of adjustments are taking location around the sector due to ICT enabled governance. As those adjustments are going on very unexpectedly, corporations have a tendency to adopt ICT at the same pace and velocity to stay in the competitive marketplace. Many research has undertaken to assess the effect evaluation on the subject of fee, pleasant, revenue generation, and perceived price introduced to the clients, but very little studies has undertaken to assess the impact in terms of the employees.

KEYWORDS: governance, employees, information, communication, technology

INTRODUCTION

Electronic governance or e-governance is the utility of statistics and communique generation for turning in authorities services, change of information, communique transactions, integration of diverse stand-alone structures and offerings among authorities-to-citizen, government-to-enterprise.E-Governance is commonly understood as the use of Information and Communication Technology at all of the degree of the Government if you want to provide offerings to the citizens, interaction with business firms and conversation and trade of information among distinctive companies of the Government in a speedy, convenient green and obvious manner(van Dijck 2013).E-governance has gained extra recognition in convoluted business international. Many management pupils have defined the idea of e governance which is emerging as an crucial activity within the enterprise discipline. It is mounted that E-governance is the application of facts and communique technologies to transform the efficiency, effectiveness, transparency and duty of informational and transactional exchanges within government, between authorities & government. Businesses of National, State, Municipal and Local ranges, citizen & groups, and to empower residents via access & use of facts. E-governance can best be viable if the authorities are prepared for it. It isn't a sooner or later venture, and so the government has to make plans and implement them before switching to it. Some of the measures encompass(Fung, Garcia-Herrero, and Ng, n.d.) Investment in telecommunication infrastructure, price range resources, make sure safety, screen assessment, internet connectivity velocity, sell focus amongst public concerning the importance, aid from all government departments and so on .E-governance has a exceptional position to play, that improves and supports all responsibilities done through the government department and organizations, because it simplifies the project on the one hand and will increase the fine of labor on the other.E-Governance is thought as the usage of Information and Communication Technology (ICT) at all the degree of the Government so that you can provide offerings to the citizens, interaction with business. businesses and verbal exchange and alternate data between extraordinary companies of the Government in a speedy, handy green and obvious manner. Users can locate distinct information about e-Governance, National Conference on e-Governance, GATI e-services, awards scheme, etc.(Earley 2014). Mobile governance (m-governance) portal also known as Mobile Seva affords an integrated platform for shipping of government services to citizen over cellular gadgets the use of SMS, USSD, IVRS, CBS, LBS, or cell programs established at the mobile phones. Users can access cell apps stores, eSMS carriers and so on. Articles and movies associated with mobile governance are also available. Information approximately Mobile Seva Portal:Mobile Seva is an innovative initiative aimed toward mainstreaming cellular governance (m-Governance) inside the us of a. The portal is controlled by using the Department of Electronics and Information Technology (DeitY), Ministry of Information and Technology. Uses can get statistics about the diverse citizen services which includes SMS, USSD, IVRS, and so on. Supplied thru cellular governance. User guide, demo video, presentation, ebook info, etc. Information on National e-Governance Plan. The National e-Governance Plan (NeGP) has been formulated by way of the Department of Information Technology (DIT) and Department of Administrative Reforms & Public Grievances (DARPG). The NeGP objectives at enhancing transport of Government services to citizens and organizations. You can get particular records on offerings, projects, know-how portals, and so on. Information associated with Service Delivery Gateway, Common Service Centre, State Data Centre. Aim of these study e-governance will reduce the work burn of government workers.

OBJECTIVE

- This paper analyses that e governance will reduce the work burn of government workers,
- To study about e-governance.
- To find out the impact on e-governance.
- One of the basic objectives of e-governance is to make every information of the government available to all in the public interest.

<u>REVIEW OF LITERATURE</u>

(Bwalya and Joseph 2012)This study analyzes and examines in certain the impact of e-governance on the economic system of Pakistan. This research additionally focuses on the manner with the aid of that every citizen can touch the authorities via a website in which all bureaucracy, law, information and different facts may be available. In close to future maximum transactions may be done at an ATM, by using mail or by way of the Internet, which has stored banks full-size expenses.(Jalal 2014)India, the growing economic wonderful-power proceeded with lightning pace toward the adoption and a hit implementation of e-governance. The Government of West Bengal (federal unit of India) carried out e-governance in pension office eg:Pension Management System (PMS), for quicker and green shipping of public offerings. The success of PMS is dependent on many factors and considered one of them is the a success adoption with the aid of the employee which has been empirically analyzed(United Nations 2018)Progress in online service delivery maintains in most nations around the arena. The United Nations e Government Surveys record that, many nations have put in location e Government projects and information and communique technologies applications for the humans to further enhance public region efficiencies and streamline governance structures to aid sustainable improvement.(Kettani and Moulin 2015)In recent years, Internet and Information Technology increase has been the principal driving force and catalyst for call for of change in most of the enterprise and carrier sectors in the global. There from, new technology and ideas has modified government interaction with commercial enterprise, agencies, businesses and citizens by way of setting up new provider styles, which includes: e-banking, e-trade, e-voting Etc.(Kettani and Moulin 2015) The essential concept of e-government is to outline the use of to be had facts and communication technology infrastructure to be able to transform government services from traditional manner to more on hand, effective and accountable carrier way.(Cowen 2011)Information and Communication Technology nowadays has become a vital component in our lives, gaining extensive software in human activities. This is because of the fact that, its use is much less expensive, more comfy, and lets in rapid data transmission and get right of entry to.(Geertz 2017)This paper takes an overview study of e-governance, one of the most annoying programs of facts and conversation era for public services. The paper summarizes the concept of e-governance, its major essence and a few ongoing e-governance sports in a few elements of the world. (Misuraca 2007)This paper is a summary of e-governance, its essence and e-governance latest sports in some elements of the sector. We have made a modest effort to give e-governance as a idea and discover the maximum fundamental of its goals and goals. We see that the good effects of e-governance may be carried out in any organized frame where human beings must be controlled thru, records sharing and communique using the net as a medium. (Bwalya and Joseph 2012)E-Governance is set reform in governance, facilitated with the aid of the creative use of Information and Communication Technology (ICT). This results in better get admission to to statistics and high-quality services for residents. Government invests massive sums of money in implementing e-governance tasks for reaping rewards the residents. The predominant objective in the back of e-governance is to offer assist and simplify governance for citizens. (Graycar and Villa 2011)The gift paper discusses the advantages of e-governance through reviewing the preceding studies performed through numerous researchers. The researches at the advantages of e-governance in the contexts of diverse growing and advanced countries are reviewed. (Nugroho 2017)This paper is Based on the evaluate of earlier studies, a framework for categorizing the benefits of e- governance is proposed inside the context of India, wherein 4 dimensions of advantages are identified. (Alberti, Klarskov, and United Nations. Dept. of Economic and Social Affairs 2006)Effective e-government is becoming an essential goal for plenty governments round the arena Within this context this paper objectives to check and reorganize the preceding paintings about e-authorities inclusive of e-authorities definition, sorts, advantages and barriers to e-government. It gives crucial heritage knowledge to the research issue, in addition to highlighting the primary standards of e-government (L. Warren and Warren 2018)This paper highlights the position and capability of records and conversation technology in helping the best governance programs in growing countries. ICTs can make a full-size contribution to the success of proper governance goals. This e-governance makes the governance extra green and extra effective, and also brings benefits to the residents of the United States of America. (Balasubramanian 2013)This paper discusses the elements which can be answerable for good governance, e-authorities initiatives in exceptional states of India, and also consists of a few present day demanding situations for coping with E-Government initiatives in India. This paper also consists of the contemporary status of E- Governance in

India. (Luccock 1809)This paper compares the issued hints with the associated hints of different global locations in phrases of account manipulate, employee's access, worker behavior, ideal use, safety, content material cloth, felony problems, and citizen conduct and it additionally enumerates its scope, deserves, and demerits for further enhancements. (Keating and Chou 1984)Information and communications generation or statistics and communique generation, usually called ICT, is frequently used as an prolonged synonym for records era (IT) allied with the pc and communication resources. It changed into treated as an digital technique to storage, retrieval and processing on numerous sorts of statistics. (Compendium of E-Governance Initiatives in India 2008)The reason of this paper is to explore E-Governance in Punjab which is the richest nation of India. However, it is a regular mission to explore integrated E-governance in Punjab, however this paper will try to represent the everything of E-governance in Punjab with protection factor of view. Thus, this paper will talk from introductory definition of E-governance to applied key initiatives beneath E-governance with safety.

MATERIALS AND METHOD:The aim of the study is to study on E-GOVERNANCE WILL REDUCE THE WORKBURN OF THE GOVERNMENT WORKER .The study is based on both secondary and primary data for the study was collected from 200 sample respondents by using a well structured questionnaire. The sampling method used in the study convenient sampling. The independent variables are age,gender,occupation,place of living and educational qualification and dependent variable is public opinion on "E-GOVERNANCE WILL REDUCE THE WORKBURN OF THE GOVERNMENT WORKER

RESULT AND ANALYSIS

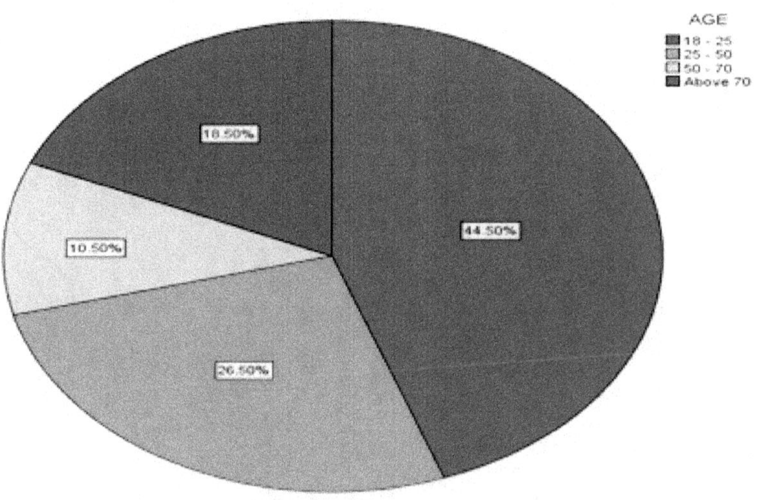

LEGENDS: Figure 1 showing the age distribution of samples respondents

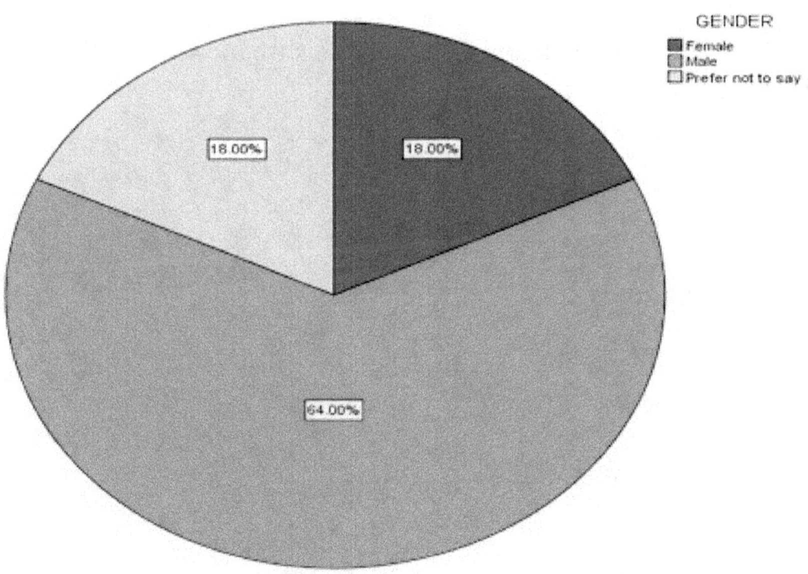

LEGEND: Figure 2 showing the gender distribution of samples respondents

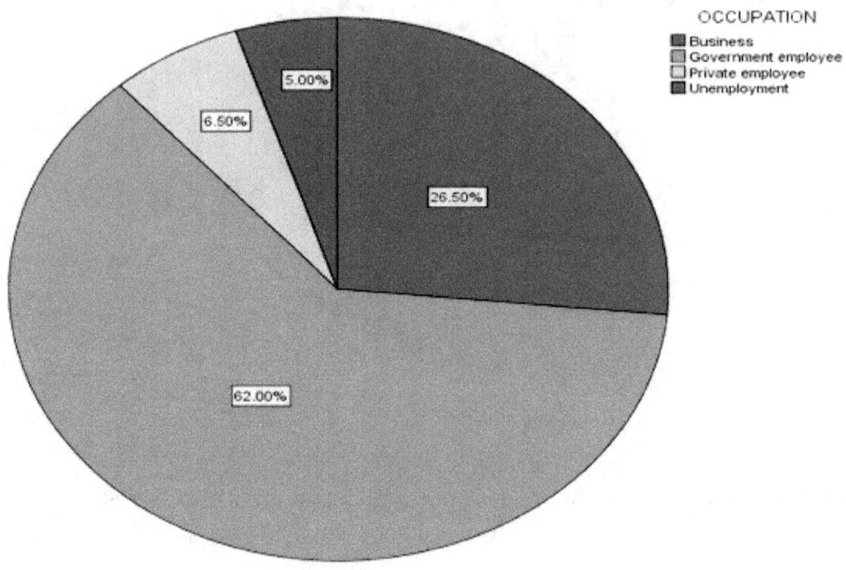

LEGEND: Figure 3 showing the occupation distribution of samples respondents

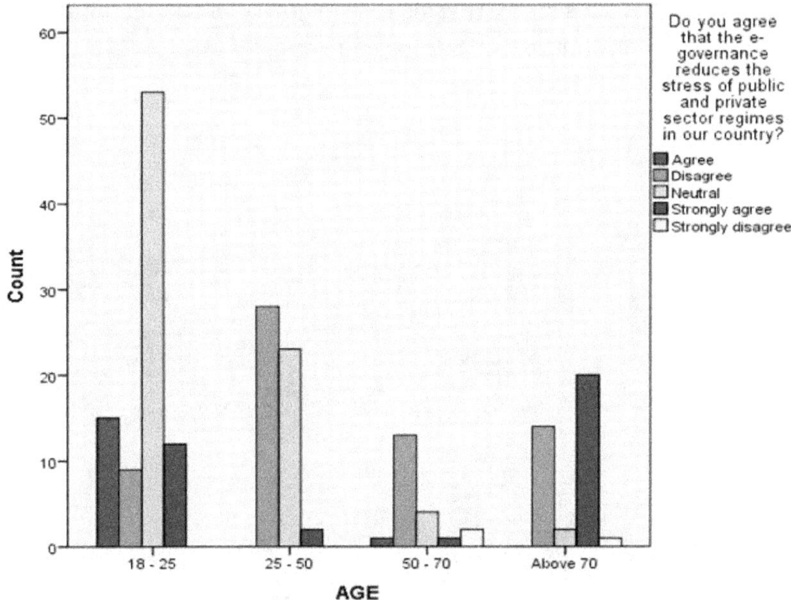

LEGEND: Figure 4 This study reveals that majority of the respondents agre with above statement it reduces the workburn of the government employee.

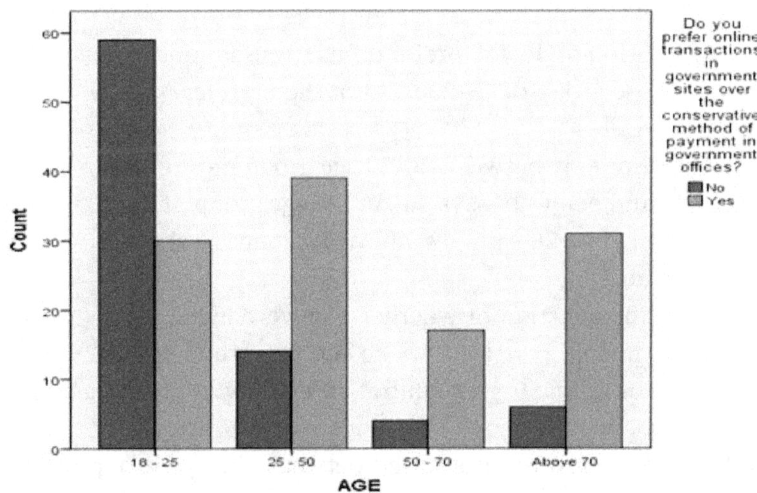

LEGENT: figure 5 This study reveals that majority of the respondents prefer online transaction.mostly 18-25 age group.

Result

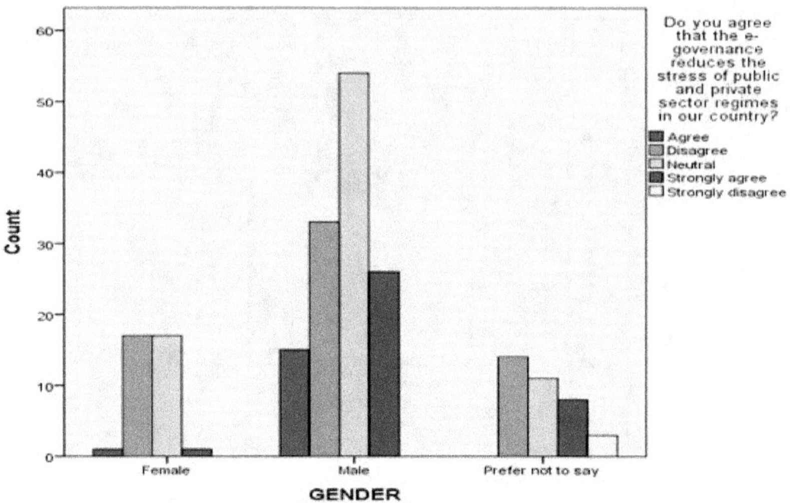

LEGEND: figure 6 This study reveals that majority of the respondents e governance reduces the stress of the public and private sector

RESULT

Table 1 The question of do you prefer online transactions in government sites people in the age group of 18-25 most of them prefer No and 30 count prefer yes.

Table 2 In the same way between 20-50 age group most of them says yes that is count of 40 and below 10 says no , in the age group of 50-70 very less people says no and below 20 says yes, above 70 count of above 30 says yes and below 10 says no.

Table 3 Result The question of whether e- governance reduces stress of private and public people People between the age group of 18-25 mostly people about the count of 50 stay neutral and below 20 count agree and below 10 count disagree and above 10 count strongly agree.

Table 4 The same question was raised between the age group of 25-50 below 30 count agree and between 20-30 count agree between the age group of 50-70 people below 20 agree and people below 10 are neutral and people between the age group of 70 and above below 20 agree and above 20 strongly agree.

Table 5 The study of e- governance reduces the stress of the public and private sector. It makes the work of the people very easy and useful. It is implementing various projects with the objective of making all Government services, wherever feasible & accessible to the common man.

Table 6 In this diagram female both agree and disagree equally and in the same way most of them are neutral and many strongly agree and very few disagree. In the same way when the question of e-governance was asked some prefer not to say and many agree and few disagree.

DISCUSSION : This study reveals that the majority 44.50%of the respondents belong to age group between 18-25.18%of the respondents are belongs to age group between above 70.This study reveals that majority64% of the respondents are male.18%of the respondents are female.remaining 18%of the respondents are not prefer to say. This study reveals that majority 62%of the respondents are government employee.26%of the respondents are doing business.

This study reveals that the majority of the respondents agree with the above statement it reduces the workburn of the government employee. This study reveals that majority of the respondents prefer online transaction.mostly 18-25 age group .This study reveals that majority of the respondents e governance reduces the stress of the public and private sector. This study reveals that the majority of the respondents e governance reduces the stress of public and private sector. I always prefer online transactions in government sites over the conservative method of payment in government offices. Nearly 58 percent of people below the age group 18-25 has said NO and 30 percent of people of the same age have said Yes. In the same way people belonging to the age group of 25-50 nearing 40 perce nt has said Yes and only 10 percent has said No , people belonging to the age group of 50-70 less than 10 percent has said No and less than 20 percent has said Yes, people above 70 nearly 30 percent has said Yes and less than 10 percent has said No.This e-government applications have many benefits for citizens, businesses, and government sectors to access to available government information 24 hours a day.Seven days a week which improves the quality of these sectors. E-government will lead to reduction of customers and organisations time , effort and costs, that will lead to improvement of service delivery and citizens satisfaction. Increase of users ICT skills internet knowledge and computer usage , creation of new business and work opportunities. It improves efficiency of government agencies in processing of data. Improves services through better understanding of users requirements thus aiming for seamless online services.

LIMITATION

The major limitation of my studies is the sample frame. The sample frame is an online based questionnaire here .The restriction of sample size is also another major drawback. The physical factors are what is the most impactful and a major factor limiting the study. The reacher cannot be able to go directly and know about the opinion of the people , via online by using social media only the reacher is able to contact people and know about their opinion this is one of the major drawbacks.

CONCLUSION

This study related to e governance will reduce the work burn of government workers.yes it is definitely reduce the work burn and also its is easy method to pay the money.reduce the time it's is applicable at everywhere and everyplace.Governance and Good Governance are compelling concepts, and might get even higher prominence within the future. The standards are firmly installed on the international time table, and a debate is in progress on their refinement and applicability. This ongoing debate is one wherein all countries and applicable stakeholders, and not only some essential players, should participate to ensure that the principles are nicely defined and applicable.this study we use empirical research method.

CHAPTER THREE

SAMPLING, REPLAY/ INTERPOLATION, MASHUPS IN THE MUSIC AND ENTERTAINMENT LAW

Author: Abhinav Pandey, III year of B.A., L.L.B. (Hons.) from University of Lucknow

Introduction

The technique of Digital Copying a piece of an existing recording and placing this "Sample" into a new recording is known as sampling. Despite the huge popularity of such songs, there is an imposing threat to copyright infringers who without prior permission of the original song makers the sound recording artist, the lyricist, the music composer, incorporates the material part of the pre-existing song in their musical work. In case, a refashioned song is made available on a commercial platform without taking license from the original creators, the song maker can be held liable for infringing copyright primarily. Even the websites which provides a platform to the primary infringers and uploads their pirated works can be held liable as secondary copyright infringers. Though copyright infringement is per se illegal irrespective of the damage caused, it is quite evident that more the refashioned song gets popular, enabling extraction of huge commercial benefits, the probability of facing a lawsuit becomes high.The amount of appropriation required for actionable copying, on the other hand, is still unknown. More than that, sampling music has transformed the way music is made. The issue arises when some musicians use the universal exception of "Fair Use" to justify the violation of copyrighted music.

Composition and Sound Recording Copyrights

In a 1952 issue of the Chicago Daily Tribune, journalist Will Leonard described the idea of covering a song as "trade jargon meaning to record a tune that looks like a potential hit on someone else's label". There are also several concerns on the part of the original music composers that companies making cover versions, remixes and music videos of their compositions are debasing the compositions. In the case of The Gramophone Company of India Ltd vs. Super Cassette Industries, the Hon'ble Judge has remarked,A version recording, we are told, is a sound recording made of an already published song by using another voice or voices and with different musicians and arrangers. Version recording is thus neither copying nor reproduction of the original recording". Infringing copy" with reference to a sound recording, which is relevant, is defined under Section 2(m) (iii), thus: "infringing copy" means,- in relation to a sound recording, any other recording embodying the same sound recording, made by any means. Section 13 defines the works in which copyright subsists. It provides that copyright shall not subsist in any sound recording made in respect of a literary, dramatic or musical work, if in making the sound recording; copyright in such work has been infringed. Section 14 specifies the content of the rights comprised in the "copyright." Section 14(e) of the Copyright Act deals with sound recordings.

The Copyright Amendment Act, 2012

The Copyright Amendment Act, 2012 brought in a phenomenal change with respect to the rights of music directors, lyricists and performers. Section 31C of the Copyright Amendment Act, 2012 deals with statutory licenses that can be obtained for making a sound recording in respect of any literal, dramatic or musical work. "Cover version" means a sound recording made in accordance with the above-mentioned section. There can be two forms of licenses that legalise this action i.e. Statutorylicenses and General licenses. While a statutory license is governed by the provisions of this Act, a general license is made on the terms and conditions as agreed upon between the licensor and licensee. This section also lays down various other rules which one has to abide by while making a cover. The person making the sound recordings should give prior notice of his intention to make the sound recordings.

Copyright Protection in Musical Work

Section 2 (P) of the Copyright Act

Music work is defined underSection 2 (P) of the copyright act of 1957 and includes works composed of music and containing graphic symbols. The original song is Formalised, Modified and Transferred to the category of the original work. Use sound to create new music by Adding, Mixing and Deleting certain aspects of the original song.

Section 52 (1) (j)

Section 52 (1) (j) stipulates that specific uses and modifications of works such as music and sound recordings require the copyright owner's consent. It constitutes a legal license to use a copyrighted work in a certain way, provided that the user pays the necessary fees and complies with the law.

Gramophone Co v. Super Cassettes

In the Case of Gramophone Co v. Super Cassettes, the court held that obtaining the assent of the original owner of a piece of music is essential. The court gave the opposite view in the case of Gramophone Co v. Mars was that so long as the situations of section 52 (1) (j) of the act are followed, there might be no infringement, there isn't any necessity of acquiring an assent. Super Cassette Industries limited v. Bathla Cassette Industries. The Court has decided not to change the singer's vocal performance because it is an integral part of the song and cannot be changed, not including prior consent of the owner of a musical work according to section 52 (1) (j).

Section 57 of the Copyright Act

Section 57 of the Copyright Act defines moral rights. Amar Nat Sagal v. Union of India, it has been determined that the author's moral rights are the lifeblood of his plant. You have the right to conserve, guard and develop your works, whether they belong entirely or partly protected by copyright.Although the world of music copyright law is quite complicated, it is not difficult to protect a piece of music and collect royalties for it, at least not mechanically. All you have to do is register your copyright, join the necessary debt collection agency and choose a distributor.

Music Sampling

Sampling is the process of using portions of an existing audio recording in a new recording. Samples can be anything that has been recorded, including music, dialogue, sound effects and more. Samples can be used in a variety of ways: as musical accompaniment for an entirely new track, as snippets of spoken or sung phrases or simply as atmosphere or texture. While sampling is most associated with hip-hop, the technique is also used in many other genres of music.

Sampling was originally developed by experimental musicians working with musiqueconcrète and electroacoustic music. These musicians would sample audio by physically manipulating tape loops or vinyl records on a phonograph. It has since evolved into a musical language that almost defines today's pop culture. Much of today's popular music contains samples from other songs.

Music Sampling in US

The US deals with music sampling a bit differently. In the US, the doctrine of fair use can be applied. The defence of 'fair use' is very limited and can be used only in specific purposes which includes parody, criticism, news reporting, research, education and similar non-profit use.

Acuff-Rose Music v. Campbell

The US Supreme Court reversed the decision of lower court stating that the use of pre-existing work in a new song could be 'fair' and what is fair has to be construed according to the facts of each case.

Mashups

A Mashup is a piece of recorded music that is comprised entirely of samples taken from other recordings and remixed to create a single new track. A standard mashup encompasses sample from two or more pre-existing songs, involving different artists, integrated into one track by manipulation of elements like tempo and pitch of the vocals as well as the instruments. Mashups are exclusively made by combining pre-existing tracks whereas in remix, samples are combined with a new content.

What is Interpolation?

Interpolation is more prevalent in the industry, and it involves taking part of a record and recreating it in another record. Imagine it like seeing a chair you like and getting someone to make a similar chair for you to put in your living room, instead of buying that exact chair for your living room. Since clearing samples is quite expensive and takes a lot of process, artists have taken to interpolating records, which obtaining permission for is quite easier. For interpolation, you only need to get permission from the original composer of the melody you are interpolating.Though rare, the owner of the record may refuse to grant permission for you to sample or interpolate their records. It is important to note that sampling or interpolating without express permission from the owner is intellectual property theft and could result in a major lawsuit against you or the artiste sampling a record.

The US Circuit Court and the Future of Sampling

Litigation over sampling has been a reality for over 50 years but for much of that history, the controversy has concerned very significant and obvious samples.Perhaps the most famous of such cases is Campbell v. Acuff-Rose Music, Inc., better known as the "Pretty Woman" lawsuit. In that case, Acruff-Rose Music, rightsholders to the Roy Orbison song Oh, Pretty Woman, sued 2 Live Crew and their label over their song Pretty Woman. 2 Live Crew had heavily sampled the original, including drum, bass and guitar riffs but claimed that the song was a parody. The case would eventually make it to the Supreme Court in 1994, which ruled that the sampling was a fair use, creating a standard that has gone on to be a key one in many fair use cases to come. More recent cases, however, have focused on smaller and smaller samples. At the forefront of that push has been TufAmerica, a company that has acquired the rights to a large number of songs used in samples and has aggressively filed lawsuits over them, sometimes without the knowledge or participation of the sampled performers/composers. For example, in 2012, TufAmerica filed a lawsuit against Jay Z alleging the rapper's 2009 song Run This Town sampled illegally from Hook and Sling Part One by singer-pianist Eddie Bo due to a sampled "Oh". That lawsuit was dismissed in 2014 when the judge ruled that one syllable didn't qualify for copyright protection. Jay-Z is far from alone as TufAmerica has also targeted Beastie Boys, Kanye West and Frank Ocean to name a few. Though TufAmerica has been able to secure some settlements, they haven't always succeeded in courts. Their 2012 action against the Beastie Boys for samples of the go-go band Trouble Funk, for example, failed when it was discovered that they didn't actually own the copyright. These lawsuits are aided by new software that can detect samples that, previously, were next to impossible to identify using the ears along. Additionally, websites like Who Sampled that create libraries of known samples may unwittingly help in the proces. In short, technology has made it possible to spot samples the same way that we spot reused and plagiarized text, down to snippets that would be almost impossible to detect any other way. But with the increased litigation comes increased scrutiny from the courts, and those courts haven'always aligned with the Bridgeport decision.

Doctrine of fair Use

Doctrine of fair use is a defense to copyright infringement that allows restricted use of copyrighted work without the owner' s permission. Fair use doctrine was fabricated in order to protect the right to freedom of expression for works which are precious and valuable to society. Section 52 xvii of Indian Copyright Act deals with fair use doctrine. According to Section 107 of US copyright Act, in order to take this defense, the defendant has to qualify a four factor test the 'purpose and character of the use,'the 'nature of the copyrighted work,'the 'amount and substantiality of the portion used in relation to the copyrighted work as a whole' and, the 'effect of the use upon the potential market for or value of the copyrighted work.' Though no single factor of the fair use test is necessarily determinative, the ' ;purpose and character of the use' of the infringer' s work normally weighs heavy in the judge' s decision. If the purpose is to make a genuine parody of satire of the original musical work, the alleged infringer can be excused. This doctrine can never be easily applied as this doctrine has very narrow application and is construed according to the facts of each case. Moreover, the risk involved in taking of the defense of fair use is that once the defense fails, one will be liable for copyright infringement. If a composition is completely remodeled into a new work, such as a parody song, it can be considered to be a fair use and hence can be exempted from the liabilities. This doctrine is applicable where a work is created in order to comment and criticize a pre-existing work. However this doctrine is not reliable in case where songs are refashioned and subsequently uploaded for commercial purposes.

Conclusion

In conclusion, music sampling, making mashups and remixes can result in copyright infringement enabling the copyright holders to sue the primary as well as secondary infringers. To avoid this, before incorporating a sample of pre-recorded song into a new song, a clearance license should be obtained from the sound recorder, music composer and the lyricists and royalty fee should be paid to them. just as it is not right to take what belongs to others without their permission, the same goes with copyright law that will not permit the usage especially when financial gain is derived from such – of another person's intellectual property with the appropriate approval licence. Thus, before any sample or interpolation is done, it behoves the person who intends to make use of the work of another to get such work cleared to prevent a legal suit against him or her; financial loss and sometimes reputational damage.

CHAPTER FOUR

CONVENTION ON THE ELIMINATION OF ALL FORMS OF DISCRIMINATION AGAINST WOMEN

Author: Simran, II year of B.A.,LL.B. from Geeta Institute of Law

Co-author: Rashi Rathi, II year of B.A.,LL.B. from Geeta Institute of Law

It entered into force as an international treaty on September 3, 1981, after being ratified by a 20th country. By his 10th anniversary of the 1989 Convention, about 100 countries had agreed to be bound by its provisions. The Convention is the culmination of more than 30 years of work by her United Nations Commission on the Status of Women, established in 1946, to monitor the situation of women and promote their rights. The Commission's work has helped to clarify all areas where women are denied equality with men. These efforts to advance women have resulted in several declarations and conventionsrice field.

The Convention on the Elimination of All Forms of Discrimination against Women is its central and most comprehensive instrument.Among the international human rights treaties, the treaty occupies an important place by putting women, who make up half of humanity, at the forefront of human rights issues. The spirit of the Convention is rooted in the United Nations goal of reaffirming belief in fundamental human rights, human dignity and worth, and equality between men and women. This document explains what equality means and how it can be achieved. As such, the Convention not only creates an international charter of women's rights, but also national action plans to ensure the enjoyment of these rights. The Convention clearly acknowledges in its preamble that "extensive discrimination against women continues" and emphasizes that such discrimination is "contrary to the principle of equality and respect for human dignity".

As defined in Article 1, discrimination is defined as "any distinction, exclusion or restriction made on the basis of sex in the political, economic, social, cultural, civil orother sphere". understood. The Convention urges States parties to "take all appropriate measures, including legislation, to ensure the full development and progress of women and to guarantee the exercise and enjoyment of their human rights and fundamental freedoms on an equal basis with them. It explicitly reaffirms the principle of equality by asking us to "take action." men" (Article 3). The equality agenda is set out in a series of fourteen articles. In its approach, the Convention covers three aspects of a woman's situation. Civil rights and the status of women are discussed in detail. Furthermore, unlike other human rights treaties, this treaty also addresses aspects of human reproduction and the impact of cultural factors on gender relations. The legal status of women gets the most attention. Concerns about fundamental rights to political participation have not diminished since the 1952 Convention on the Political Rights of Women.

That provision is therefore repeated in Article 7 of this document, guaranteeing the right of women to vote, hold public office and hold public office. This includes the equal right of women to represent their countries at the international level (Article 8). The Convention on the Nationality of Married Women, passed in 1957, is incorporated into Article 9, which provides for the sovereignty of women irrespective of their marital status. The Convention thus notes that a woman's legal status is often tied to marriage, making her dependent on her husband's nationality rather than on her own rights. Articles 10, 11 and 13 each affirm women's right to non-discrimination in education, employment, economic and social activities. As referred to in Article 14, these demands regarding the situation of rural women are of particular importance, and her particular struggles and important economic contributions deserve more attention in policy making. I have. Article 15 affirms the full equality of women in civil and business matters and states that all instruments aimed at restricting women's legal and legal capacity are "deemed null and void". I am requesting. and family back relationships, exercising equal rights and duties of women and men in choosing a spouse, parental and personal rights, and disposition of assets Apart from civil rights issues, the Convention also pays close attention to a very important concern of women: women's reproductive rights. The link between discrimination and women's reproductive roles is a recurring issue of concern in the Convention. For example, in Article 5, she calls for a "proper understanding of motherhood as a social function" and calls for men and women to take full joint and several responsibilities for raising children. Therefore, provisions on maternity protection and child care have been declared essential rights and are included in all areas of the Convention, including employment, family law, core health and education. Social obligations extend to the provision of social services, particularly childcare facilities, that enable individuals to reconcile family obligations with work and participation in public life. Special maternity protection measures are recommended and "should not be considered discriminatory"(Article 4). "The Convention also affirms women's right to reproductive choices, and in particular is the only human rights treaty to mention family planning. States parties are obliged to include family planning counseling in the educational process (art. 10.h) and guarantee "the right of women to freely and responsibly determine the number and spacing of their children and to access information".

You are obliged to create family norms. Formally recognizing restrictions on women from enjoying their fundamental rights, these powers of hers are shaped into stereotypes, customs and norms, resulting in a variety of legal, political and economic Barriers to Women's Active Participation Given this interrelationship, the Preamble to the Convention stresses that "the achievement of full equality between men and women requires a change in the traditional roles of men and women in society and in the family". doing. States parties, therefore, should "enforce the social and cultural women have an obligation to work towards changing their behavioral patterns" (Article 5). And Article 10c. requires revision of textbooks, school programs and teaching methods to eliminate stereotypes in education. All provisions of the Convention affirming the equal responsibilities of men and women in family life and the equal rights to education and employment were strongly targeted. Overall, the Convention created and perpetuated gender discrimination. Implementation of the Convention is monitored by the Committee on the Elimination of Discrimination against Women (CEDAW). The powers of the Commission and the operation of the Convention are defined in Articles 17 to 30 of the Convention. The Commission is composed of 23 experts nominated by governments and elected by States parties as persons "of high moral standing and competence in the field covered by the Convention".States parties are expected to submit to the Commission, at least every four years, national reports detailing the steps they have taken to implement the provisions of the Convention. Commission members discuss these reports with government officials at their annual meetings and explore with them areas for further action in their countries. The Committee also makes general recommendations to the State party on issues related to the elimination of discrimination against women.

It is often referred to as the International Charter of Women's Rights. Consisting of a preamble and 30 articles, it defines what constitutes discrimination against women and sets an agenda for national action to end such discrimination. The Convention defines discrimination against women as: Respect for equality, human rights and fundamental freedoms between men and women, whether political, economic, social, cultural, civil or otherwise" Commit to take many steps to end forms of discrimination against women Integrate the principle of gender equality into the legal system, repeal all discriminatory laws and pass appropriate laws prohibiting discrimination against women Yes Establish courts and other public institutions Establish facilities to ensure effective social security Ensure women are protected from discrimination. Ensure the elimination of all acts of discrimination against women by individuals, organizations or businesses. The Convention achieves equality between women and men by ensuring equal access and equality of opportunity for women in political and public life, including education, health and employment, as well as the right to vote and stand for election. form the basis for States Parties agree to take all appropriate measures, including legislation and special temporary measures, to ensure that women can fully enjoy their human rights and fundamental freedoms.

The Convention is the only human rights treaty that affirms women's reproductive rights and targets culture and tradition as powerful forces shaping gender roles and family relationships. It affirms the right of women to acquire, change and retain nationality, as well as the right to retain the nationality of their children. The Parties also agree to take appropriate measures against all forms of trafficking and exploitation of women. States that have ratified or acceded to the Convention have a legal obligation to implement its provisions. We also undertake to submit, at least every four years, a country-by-country report on the steps taken to fulfill our contractual obligations.

The principal members or parties to the Convention are all United Nations Member States, with the exception of the six Member States, which have not ratified the Convention: Iran, Palau, Somalia, Sudan, Tonga, and the United States. By signing the Convention, States agree to take a series of measures to eliminate all forms of discrimination against women, including:

1.) Laws prohibiting discrimination against women.

2.) Establish courts and other public institutions to effectively protect women from discrimination.

3.) ensure the elimination of all acts of discrimination against women by individuals, organizations or businesses;

The Convention aims to recognize all forms of discrimination against women in the civil, political, social, economic, legal and cultural life of each country.

Furthermore, it seeks to ensure equal treatment of men and women by raising awareness of the changes needed. The convention covers all aspects of women's lives. CEDAW has the Sustainable Development Goals accepted by UN leaders in 2015. With the 2030 Agenda for Sustainable Development and 17 Sustainable Development Goals (SDG), they aim for the next 15 years (SDG). This agenda aims to achieve gender equality by empowering women and eliminating all forms of discrimination against them. Gender equality has received a lot of attention in the pursuit of sustainable development and is linked to all SDGs.Leaders, along with the SDGs and CEDAW, will join forces with the Human Rights Foundation to ensure gender equality, empower all girls and women, and address and implement accountability measures to combat all forms of discrimination. was established.

<u>Authors' Bio</u>

I am Simran. I am basically from Panipat, Haryana. Let me tell you about my Schooling. I studied at Arya Bal Bharti Public School, Panipat. I am currently pursuing B.A.LL.B (2nd year) from Geeta institute of law which is approved by: Bar Council of India and affiliated to Kurukshetra university. But I don't want to be a lawyer...I am much more interested in some other work like legal advisor, IAS or crack judiciary exam. My hobbies are reading interesting facts, writing blogs, articles, research paper and helping needy person. Recently I read about Convention on the elimination of all forms of Discrimination Against women and then I write a blog about this. So that was about me and my blog.

DE FACTO MARRIAGE:Live-IN- RELATIONS: UNMARRIED COUPLES: RIGHTS AND OBLIGATIONS

Author: Arjun Maheshwari, I year of B.A.,LL.B.(Hons.) from Dr. Ram Manohar Lohiya National Law University

What are Live- relationships in India, and what are their Provisions?

It is described as "An arrangement or cohabitation in which two people are involved in a sexual and romantic relationship and are living as partners (Husband & Wife) in the same house or place and showing society that they are couples without marriagefor a long time."In this, the couples show that they depend on each other but do not want to carry out the marriage rituals.

In this kind of relationship,couples do not feelthe need to carry out marriage rituals. Still, when the connectiongetsbroken,either one of them (especially women) or both have to suffer a lot because they do not have the rights that a married couple has.

What are its Provisions and rulings

1. According to the Report of 2003 related to Reforms of the Criminal Justice System (spearheaded by Dr Justice V.S. Malimath), which gave two recommendations –

- The evidence regarding a man and woman living together for a sufficiently long period should be enough to draw the presumption that the marriage was performed according to the customary rites and ceremonies of the parties,
- Thus, it is proposed that the word wife in section 125 of CrPC should be altered to include a woman living with the man like his wife for a reasonably protracted period.

The second point that the report raises is to amend the definition of wife under section 125 of CrPC and to include women who live as a wife with someone.

2. Protection of Women from Domestic Violence Act, 2005, section 2(f) Definition travels outside the confines of a marital relationship and even includes live-inrelationshipslike marriage

3. According to the Law of Presumption of Marriage (a judicial pronouncement), the law will presume in favour of marriage where a couple has been living like a husband and wife for a very long time.

4. According to the American Court ruling in Marvin v. Marvin which SC of Californiacoined a new expression of Palimony which is a combination of 'pal' and 'alimony'.

5. According to the SC ruling in Gokal Chand v. Parvin Kumari, 1952, the court held that continuous cohabitation of men and women as husband and wife might raise the presumption of marriage; thehusband will have the right to demolish that presumption.

6. In CHANMUNIYA V. VIRENDRA KUMAR SINGH KUSHWAHA & ANR, 2011 in which SC said three things

Presumption of marriage in favour of the wife.

The standard of Proof cannot be strict.

Where is the Conflict in law?

Conflicts in law arise from the following cases of SC ;

1. In Yamunabhai Anantrao Adhav v. Anantrao Shivram Adhav and another, 1988, SC held that the expression wife in section 125 of CrPC should be interpreted to mean only a legally wedded wife.

2. In Dwarika Prasad Satpathy v. Bidyut Prava Dixit &Anr, 1999 which SC gave the opposite ruling from the 1988 case that First, the standard of Proof of marriage in a Section 125 proceeding is not as strict as is required in a trial for an offence under Section 494 of IPC and Second where evidenceis there which shows that the couples are living as husband and wife then plea for maintenance cannot be ignored.

3. Next, in the case of Chanmuniya v. Virendra Kumar Singh Kushwaha & ANR, 2011, the womanlivedas a wife with a man. However,after a few years, the men refuseto accept the woman as his wife. The matter went to the Trial Court,whichsaid the womanwas the husband's wifeandentitled to maintenance. The case then went to the HC, which reversed the order of the Trial Court and gave the reasons that the requirements of the Hindu Marriage Act were not met.The matter then went to the SC, whichreferred to the 2011 judgment, but due to the contradictory decision of the SC in the past, the bench directedthe case to the three-judge court, which is pending till now.

4. In the case of Indra Sarma vs V.K.V.Sarma, 2013, SC said thatmarried couples are assigspecifictain responsibilities andthatlife in a relationship is like a mutual understanding and can end at anytime. Thereforeall who live in a relationship are notmarried and thus give the following guidelines:

- Reasonable period to continue the relationship
- Shared household
- Showing society that they are husband and wife

Conclusion

Hence, there is a long gap in judicial opinions. Still, there is a presumption in favour of marriage, and the person who had taken advantage of de facto marriage cannot walk freely from the social obligation.

Author's Bio

My name is Arjun Maheshwari. I am a first-year law student at NLU, Lucknow, interested in legal research and writing. I like to make productive videos and vlogs on my youtube channel.

PERSONALITY RIGHTS: SIGNIFICANCE AND ROLE IN PRESENT WORLD

Author: Aryant Pal, III year of B.A.,LL.B.(Hons.) from Banaras Hindu University

Introduction

People in India are heavily influenced by advertisements that feature celebrities. It is not limited only to costly items like diamonds and jewelleries endorsed by Amitabh Bachchan but also to small things of daily use such as energy drinks endorsed by ViratKohli. In such a case the image of that celebrity is linked to a particular product and the product is identified by his name. So it becomes very crucial for the celebrity to choose the right product for endorsement. In such a situation, it would be very disastrous for a celebrity, if someone uses his name or image or any of his characteristics, without his permission. Apart from the loss of fame the celebrity may also suffer economic loss. Hence it becomes important to understand what are personality rights and their related aspects.

What are personality rights?

Personality rights are the unique characteristics of an individual with which he is identified and upon which he has certain rights. These may be his voice, his photograph, his way of singing, or any particular way of orating a line or dialogue. In simple words, personality rights can be defined as the personality traits of a celebrity that cannot be misused by others. It is a right in rem i.e. it can be claimed against the world at large.

Why in News?

Recently, the famous actor and celebrity Mr. Amitabh Bachchan filed a civil suit in the Supreme Court for registering his personality rights. To be specific he wanted to register his unique style of referring to the computer as "Computer Ji" and selecting an option as "computer ji, is option prtalalagayajaaye".

From where does this right gets validity?

Eminent philosopher GWF Hegel has defined property as an extension of the personality. Thus, it is made similar to the rights that a person gets for his property. It is not defined specifically in the constitution or any statute but the courts have construed it as emerging from the Right to privacy defined under article 21 of the Constitution of India. The courts are of the view that a particular characteristic of a celebrity is a thing personal to him and the infringement of this privacy would come under article 21. In the case of ICC Development (International) Ltd. vs. Arvee Enterprises[i], the Delhi High Court held that: "The right of publicity has evolved from the right of privacy and can inhere only in an individual or in any indicia of an individual's personality like his name, personality trait, signature, voice. etc."

The personality rights to some extent also derive their validity from the Indian Copyright Act, 1957 and the Indian Trademarks Act, 1990. The civil courts also have the power under section 151 of CPC to prosecute a person for infringement of the personality rights of a celebrity. Section 151 of CPC reads "Nothing in this code shall be deemed to limit or otherwise affect the inherent power of the court to make such orders as may be necessary for the ends of justice or to prevent abuse of the process of the court." The procedural aspect of this section is mentioned under order-39, rule-1 and rule-2. Under these sections also a person is liable to pay damages to a celebrity for the infringement of his personality rights.

<u>To whom such rights are available?</u>

Personality rights are not available to each and every citizen like the Right to Freedom of Speech and Expression or the rights which are available to every person under article 21. The courts have held that "personality rights vests on those who have attained the status of celebrity." Now the question arises who can be called a celebrity? There is no objective or direct answer to this question. It depends on the facts and circumstances of each case. According to the Collins Dictionary[ii], a celebrity can be defined as "someone who is famous, especially in areas of entertainment such as films, music, writing or sport." In the case of TITAN Industries v. Ramkumar Jewellers[iii], the Delhi HC has defined the word celebrity as "a famous or well-known person who many people talk about or know about."

<u>Types of rights under its ambit</u>

Personality rights consist of two types of rights:

1. Right to Publicity: This refers to the right of a celebrity to protect his personality from being commercially exploited without his consent or agreement.

2. Right to privacy: This includes the right of a person to forbid public exhibition of his traits or personality.

<u>Why are Personality Rights required to be protected?</u>

India is a country where celebrity worship is done blindly.When the image of a product is linked to a particular celebrity, people tend to prefer that product over other similar products in the market. This phenomenon is exploited by businessmen who have agreements with the celebrities endorsing their products but in many cases, it has happened that, many businessmen use the personality traits of a celebrity for their product, without their permission, to deceive their customers. This has many-a-times resulted in cases lodged against that celebrity and sometimes they are even made to pay fines. It is for this very reason, personality rights need to be protected so that no person can use them without the consent of that celebrity.

Another reason is that these personality characteristics might be used to spread fake news. People tend to believe such voices or morphed videos because they are similar to renowned celebrities. Such means have many times been resorted to in the past by the powerful for their selfish purposes.

How can Personality Rights be protected?

For the protection of personality rights,Ashok Kumar orders can be passed by the courts at the request of the plaintiff. These are similar to the John Doe Orders followed by the courts in England. If a person has an apprehension that his personality rights are being infringed, then he can approach the courts for the passing of Ashok Kumar orders against the unidentified infringer. An Ashok Kumar order is a kind of injunction, accorded by the courts, where the state of affairs is such that an anonymous person is violating the IP rights of the IP rights owner and cannot be discerned at the time of filing the suit.[iv] Once these orders are passed the plaintiff gets a right to look for infringement and collect evidence if any and then complain against the infringer. Ashok Kumar orders are awarded ex-parte owing to the fact that the defendant is unidentifiable, and the time span is fleeting.[v]

What are the remedies available to the plaintiff in case of infringement of this right?

Since this right emanates from the right to life and personal liberty guaranteed under Article 21 of the constitution of India, a person always has the remedy to approach the court under this section to claim damages for the infringement of his right.

Another way the court can prosecute the accused is by initiating Contempt of Court proceedings against the accused. Now a question arises as to how infringement of personality rights is connected to contempt of court. Ashok Kumar order is basically an order issued by the court prohibiting the use of the personality traits of a celebrity without the permission of such personality. So, an infringement of such a right is a clear violation of court orders. Hence, the court has the right to prosecute a person under the relevant sections of contempt of court.

Another way a court can take cognizance against the infringer is under The Copyright Act, 1957. Section 13 of the act provides that this act extends to original literary, dramatic, musical, and artistic works; cinematograph films; and sound recording, and Section 14 authorises the owner of such artistic works to allow reproduction of their work. But the issue here is that, copyright is not provided to the artistic work but is provided to its creator. In this way, if someone misuses a photograph of a celebrity, infringement can only be claimed by the photographer and not the celebrity himself. A solution to this problem can be found under Section 38 of the act which provides a right to the performer over his performance.

Another way a court can take cognizance against the infringer is under the Trademarks Act, 1999. Section 2(1) allows a person to register a sign capable of being distinguishing goods and services of that person from others. So, through the medium of this section, a celebrity can claim infringement of his rights.

<u>Case Laws in this regard</u>

ShivajiRaoGaikwad v. Varsha Productions[vi]

In this case, there was a movie by the name "Main HoonRajnikant" which was actually the biography of Superstar Rajnikant. Neither the lead actor was Rajnikant and nor did they obtain permission from Rajnikant. So,Rajnikant filed a suit in the court seeking an injunction against the violation of his personality rights. The court in this case stayed the release of the movie and damages were also awarded to the plaintiff(Rajnikant).

Arun Jaitley v. Network Solutions Pvt. Ltd.[vii]

In this case, a suit was filed by famous politician ArunJaitley against a website registered by the name www.arunjaitley.com. Although,Mr.Jaitley lost the suit as the defendant's name was also ArunJaitley and he was able to prove that he kept the website's name on his name but the court made a very crucial observation. It stated that "Popularity or fame of an individual will be no different on the internet than in reality."Thus the court widened the boundary of personality right by including the internet under its ambit.

TATA Sons Ltd. &Anr v. Aniket Singh[viii]

This case is similar to the ArunJaitley case. In this case, a website was registered by the domain name www.cyrusmistry.com by the defendants and the plaintiff's name was also CryusMistry who was CEO of TATA Group of Industries. The Plaintiff claimed that his name is being used to derive profits by the defendant thus violating his personality rights. The court in this case ruled in favour of Plaintiff i.e Cyrus Mistry.

TITAN Industries v. RamkumarJwellers[ix]

In this case, an advertisement of some jwellers featured an image of famous celebrity Amitabh Bachchan and his wife Jaya Bachchan. The celebrities claimed that it was featured without their permission and hence is a violation of their personality rights. The courts in this case claimed in favour of the plaintiff.

GautamGambhir v. DAP Co. &Anr.[x]

This is the latest case in this regard. This suit was filed by the famous cricketer GautamGambhir who claimed that the defendants ran a restaurant named after him thus using his image without his permission. The court in this case ruled in favour of the defendants by stating that since the defendant's name was also GautamGambhir and by the use of his name there was no loss to the plaintiff in his game. So the defendants had not infringed any personality rights of the plaintiff and are not liable to pay any damages.

Conclusion

"What's in a name? that which we call a rose, By any other name would smell as sweet" These are the lines from Shakespeare's play Romeo and Juliet which translates as by changing the name, the characteristic doesn't change. But this doesn't seem to be prevalent in the present times. In the present times, a person through his hardwork earns name and fame and any act of a person which tarnishes such name should be prohibited. It is because of this very reason that the Consumer Protection act made legislation to protect consumers from false advertisements portraying the name or image of famous celebrities with which they have no nexus.

Author's Bio

I was born in Kanpur, Uttar Pradesh and got my Intermediate done from kanpur itself. When I was in class 5th or 6th, I was clear in my mind that I had to make my career in the legal field. Since the very beginning, legal and political matters have always attracted me. After I completed my 12th, I got admission in Banaras Hindu University. That was like a dream come true for me. My hobbies are reading, writing, travelling and exploring things around me.

CHAPTER SEVEN

FEMALE GENITAL MUTILATION

Author: Japkaran Sandhu, II year of B.B.A.,LL.B. from Geeta Institute of Law

First of all we know about female genital mutilation [FGM] is a procedure in which female genital are cut, injured or changed without any medical reason for is it to be done. This types of practice is a major concern in the world there are four types of female genital mutilation are clitoridectomys, excision infibulation, all are the harmful procedures not covered by the first three including pricking ,stretching , scraping or even use of acid to mutilates part of the genital area. There's a question arises why FGM is being procedures in all over the world in fact it is not a medical and have zero health benefits and it is also not essential religion practices then why FGM practices is to be done? When the girls are minor in the age in that age FGM is practiced because to prevent from sexual intercourse or you can say not to lose her virginity until her marriage to enhancing sexual pleasure to male. It's just for male sexual pleasure that's why FGM is performed how strange and cruel. FGM practicing is violating the rights following girls and women right to life, right to physical integrity , right to health and gender equality. How it will affect the health of women? FGM is very painful procedure it will affect the health of women in many ways mentally, physically, socially. In physically women faced many problems like pain, problem in menstruate, problems urinating, infectionand complication in child birth. In mentally women's are suffering from anxiety, low self-esteem, post-traumaticstress, mood disorders and in socially it is also a socialtaboo also.

COUNTRIES WITH THE HIGEST RATE OF FGM

Somalia is the main United States in FGM with 98% of ladies among the long time of 15 and forty nine years present process the exercise. Guinea, Djibouti, and Egypt additionally have extra than 90% in their ladies among the equal a long time going for circumcision. However, Egypt has the very best quantity of ladies who've gone through FGM with a complete of 27.2 million ladies accompanied through Ethiopia (23.eight million), Nigeria (19.nine million), and Sudan (12.1 million). Gambia is the main United States with the chance of a woman being circumcised due to the fact her mom become circumcised with 72% of the ladies prone to FGM. In those nations, the bulk of the ladies have been reduce earlier than their 5th birthday through a conventional practitioner. Most of them had their genitalia reduce with a few flesh removed. Social attractiveness is stated because the predominant motive and contributing component to FGM in maximum of those nations.

WOMENS SUPPORT AND WORLD VIEW

In maximum nations wherein FGM/Cutting is common, the bulk of ladies and ladies suppose that the exercise must be encouraged. In Benin and Ghana, 93% of the ladies and ladies are in aid of FGM/C. Also, in Kenya, Iraq, Niger, Togo, Burkina Faso, and Tanzania, over 85% of ladies and ladies aid the exercise. However, the exercise has the least aid amongst ladies and ladies in Guinea, Sierra Leone, Mali, and Gambia wherein much less than 30% of the ladies aid the exercise.

FEMALE GENITAL MUTILATION IN INDIA

Female genital mutilation is not legalised in India. FGM is also practised in India byDawood bohra Muslim community is a set of one million people in India, 75% of bohra community followed this practices in India as well as smaller bohra like Suleimani and alavi bohras.

SAHIYO ORGANIZATION

A women named Fatima was experienced that horrible practice she is the older sister of insia Dariawala and later she was co-founder of Sahiyo organization and four other women's with her because impact of FMG practice Dariawala avoided FGM because her mother took stand against FGM practice when she knows about what happened with Fatima. Sahiyo is the one of leading organization to stop the FGM practices

ROLE OF MUSLIM dariawala noted that female genital mutilation is not a pre Islamic practise. It is not followed by all Islamic group, in fact QURAN the holy book of Islam does not mention it. However, the daim al-Islam a religious text that bohra community can follow this practices.

<u>Why India becomes hub of FMG?</u>

Because bohra community spread over western countries like Pakistan, India, Yemen, east Africa and in some part of America and Australia In India bohra community divided in two sect Sunnis and Shias they were found in Rajasthan, Madhya Pradesh, Gujrat, Maharashtra.

India is now becoming a hub of FGM because legal action taken by Australia and America against FMG, Australia sentenced 15 month jail to 3 dawoodi bohras in case female genital mutilation in 2016 and united states of America arrested two doctors in cutting of female reproductive part of six girl in 2017.

<u>CONCLUSION</u>

Female genital mutilation is a very horrible experienced that are faced by women's in all over world FGM is violating the rights of women's in the Age of growing, learning and doing fun activities. In that age some community thinks that doing such practices is hygienic and religion practices in fact it is not written in QURAN the holly book of religion giving that pain to women is a good for just giving virgin female and pure sexual pleasure to male I think this practices should be banned by all over world it is also not a medical procedure it will done by bohra community head. I shocked to hear that in some countries women's are in support of FGM. In India FGM is also practising by some community it should be banned by law this types of hilarious practices we want's rights of women women's have rights to live freely, women has their own choice what they want, Right to life and physical integrity, Right of child. According to the UNICEF data 200 MILLION GIRLS IN 30 COUNTRIES are undergoing the process of FGM and EVERY YEAR ALMOST 3 MILLION GIRLSand WOMENS ON THE RISK OF FEMALE GENITAL MUTILATION.

CHAPTER EIGHT

PUBLIC OPINION ON INCREASING SCHOOL DROPOUT

Author: Ieswarya.N, V year of B.A.,LL.B.(Hons.) from Saveetha School of Law

Abstract

School dropout is withdraw from school , the education is basic requirement to enhance once income , talent and knowledge, Article 21A of constitution, RTE act 2010 , states about free and compulsory education to curtail dropout of students, The Union ministry of Human Resource development deals with new policies related to education,mid day meal schemes and various schemes by government to retain students and reduce dropout of students . Objective of the study analyse problems faced by dropout students , opportunities that are available to dropout students, the economic condition of dropout students , To analyze the dropout leads a student to become involved in criminal activities.The research has followed the empirical research with the convenient sampling method. The sample size covered by the researcher is 200. The independent variables are age, gender, educational qualification and occupation. The dependent variables are the reason for School dropout, dropout students involves in crime,respondents know about any dropout students.The statistical tool used here is graphical representation and pie chart distribution , the major findings include on the question the reason for dropout ,highest respondents on misleading companion and lack of parental care ,the dropout students involves in crime many answers neutral that not all dropout involves in criminal activities and many of the respondents are not known any school dropout students ,the need of better implementation of schemes and to create awareness about important of education and technology world education is much needed to sustain .Moreover education creates self confidence and it is also a right to every children.

Key words: Dropout,requirement,retain,crime,confidence.

Introduction

The education is the basic requirement for human development which ultimately increases employment opportunities increases once income level , the school dropout in India since it is very long , however the witness on massive school dropout can be clear by report of MHRD (Ministry of Human Resource development) in the year 2009-2010, which shows 20% of school dropout at Delhi in India , the enactment of Right to education act 2010 , and Article 21A by 86th constitutional amendment states free and compulsory education from 6-14 years of age as a fundamental right.The Union ministry of Human Resource development (ministry of Education) deals with new policies related to education, The Kasturba Gandhi Balika Vidyalaya Scheme to reach education to girls at minority community the scheme was implemented, the samagra Shiksha Abhigyan which enhanced students enrolment and retention of students by improving the infrastructure this scheme was enacted basis of Right to education act 2010 , the mid day meal scheme which provide food along with education increases the enrolment of students .The major factors that affects the topic are low education or illiteracy of parents leads to dropout of children,occupation of parents, large size family but low family income which is difficult for parents to maintain family as well as provide education to their children, immigration, failure in examinations feels low self esteem by students ,distance of school from home , the punishment by teachers this are the reason which increase the school dropout. The recent survey on NGOs organised by Nobel laureate Kailash satyarthi , states 85% of the organisation felt increase in school dropout in post lockdown period , these maybe due to losses household income or financial instability no proper internet facilities to attend classes leads to increase the rate of dropout ,National education policy 2020, states about the infrastructure and effective means of education and to ensure the children attend school moreover it aim to curtail school dropout.The MHRD report 2018 the dropout rate in India on upper primary is 4.13% and secondary level is 17.06% , countries like Spain the school dropout rate is 34% and in Portugal the dropout is 31%-40% the introduce of programs to reduce school dropout was worked to some extent the school dropout decrease from 40% to 32% from 2004 to 2009.The main aim of the research is to analyze the dropout leads a student to become involved in criminal activities.

Objective

To study problems faced by dropout students , to study the opportunities that are available to dropout students, to study the economic condition of dropout students , To analyze the dropout leads a student to become involved in criminal activities.

Review of literature

- In the article of " factors leading to school dropout in India" written by Sateesh Gouda explains Education Plays a vital role in human development and increases in income level of the individual as per the national family health survey 3 ,75% of the students belongs to the age group 6 to 16 years attend school out of which 14 percentage not attended the school and 11 percentage where is school dropout and the dropper categories mostly belongs to the Muslims SC /ST.(M et al,2014)

- In the article of study of "potential dropout in elementary school of Central U.P" ,written by Sabates briefs The factors are the problems relating to not attending the schools it may be the Indian education system structure or due to the poverty and illiteracy of the parents and the lack of preschool experiences, frustration of the students and the lack of achievement leads a student to drop their school .(Sabates et al,2013).

- In the article of "The enrolment and the dropout percentage of boys and girls in India" written by Ramesh Pandita Explains the secondary data collection of Ministry of human resources and development in the year of 2010 to 11 almost 78.40 % of boys and 81.72 % of the girls dropout before they are reaching the secondary level of education and the population size, socio-economic conditions and Indian education system results as per the author view .(Pandita,2015).

- In the article "The dropout among the boys and girls in U.P" written by Pandey, Gauri explains education can be withdrawn either by the transfer of one school to the other school or by the death and the lack of attendance age and the compulsory schooling which affects socially the students.(Pandey,2012).

- The article of "educational deprivation among women in the ruler area" written by Saravanan explains the need for the education of parents ,distance of schools from the home increases dropout rate of girls as per survey in Kolli Hills Namakkal districts in Tamil Nadu. (Saravanan,2015).

- In the article of risk factors for school dropout in juvenile offenders,written by Asuncion Fernandez , briefs the school dropout causes different levels of behavioural differences in the family and the neighbourhood and resulting deviant attitude irresponsibility can also engage in alcohol abuse and became and also become an juvenile offender on the analysis of the Spain in 2012.(Fernández-Suárez et al,2016).

- In the article of dropping out of high school written by Jeremy Burrus , explains The dropping is quitting the course and fails to complete the school and the major factors are like very poor graduation rates and a well planned behaviour. (Dropping Out of High School: Prevalence, Risk Factors, and Remediation Strategies,Burrus,2012).

- In the article of school dropout and offending written by Liu, explains The dropout became delinquents and became offenders to smaller extent while the non dropouts may have well socioeconomic status maybe intelligence.(Liu,2013).

- In the article of relationship between criminal involvement and the school dropout written by Iryna Rud , On the analysis of Netherlands the criminal involvement was 11 percentage higher on the school dropout and the major factors are like the school classmates the family and the individual has been an unobservable .(Rud et al,2018.).

- In the article "Effect of dropping out of high school on criminal behaviour"written by Terence briefs about the sociology theory deals with delinquency and dropout due to criminal behaviour and strain theory dropout behaviour increases by increase in criminal activities leads to dropout later involved in crime. (Thornberry et al,2006).

- In the article " high school dropout" written by Olof Blackman explains there is no evidence for criminal convictions and dropout among men, women who find occupations reduce criminal convictions.(Lochner,2010).

- In the study of " Socio economic determinants of primary school dropout" written by " Haroon Sajjad" on analysis of 4 municipal corporation schools at Delhi the students of vulnerable, urban poor,Muslim community there is dropout ,25% of male dropout from class I to V the reason like poverty and delay on schemes by government.([No Title],Sajjad,2021).

- In the study of " Economic effects of student dropout" written by Latif.A,Choudhary explains about education economic development vision 2030,which states that education influences productivity, enhances employment opportunities, women empowerment, reduces students dropout, reduces illiteracy rate ,and it also reduces non innovative environment.(Ai and Choudhary AI,2015).

• In the study of "Socio demographic characteristics of school dropout" written by Deepak kumar explains there is need of free and compulsory education upto 14 years of age as per constitution and briefs the handbook of education statistics 2013-14, the students 38.2% enroll in class I but not continue still class x and moreover it was based on socio demographic characteristics for example parents income , illiteracy etc... almost 90% dropout on government school from age 15-18 years . (Deepak,2016)

Methodology

The research method followed here is empirically rescarch .A total of 200 samples here have been taken out of which is taken through convenient sampling. The sample form taken by the researcher through online using google forms .The independent variable taken here is age ,gender and occupation and education .The dependent variables are reason for school dropout, dropout students involved in crime,respondents know any dropout students .The statistical tool used by the researcher is graphical representation and pie chart.

Analysis

Figure:1

According to you, what is the reason for school dropouts.

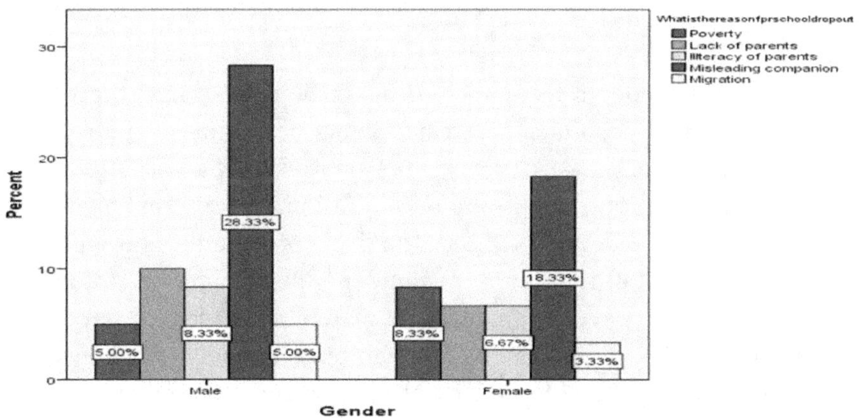

Legend : This figure deals with reasons for school dropouts with the independent variable gender .

Result : Respondents composed of both male and female answer to the question reasons for school dropouts, male respondents answered 5% on poverty, 8.3% on lack of parents and illiteracy of parents,28.3% on misleading of companion ,5% on migration and female respondents answered 8.3% on poverty ,6.67% on lack of parents and illiteracy of parents,18.3% on misleading companion and 3.3% on migration.

Figure:2

According to you, what is the reason for school dropouts.

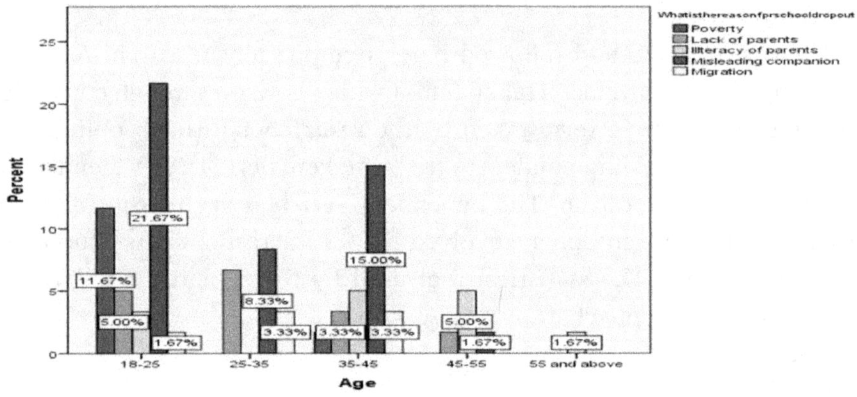

Legend : This figure deals with reasons for school dropouts with the independent variable age.

Result : Respondents from various age groups answered the question reasons for school dropouts, the respondents belonging to the age group 18-25 answers 11.67% on poverty , 5% on lack of parents , 21.67% on misleading companions and 1.67% on migration, the respondents belongs to age group 25-35 answers 8.33% on lack of parents and misleading companion, 3.33% on migration, respondents belongs to age group 35-45 answers 3.33% on poverty and lack of parents,illiteracy of parents and migration and 15% on misleading companion, respondents belongs to age group 45-55 answers 1.67 % on lack of parents and misleading companion and respondents belongs to 55 and above age answers 1.67% on illiteracy of parents.

Figure:3

According to you, what is the reason for school dropouts.

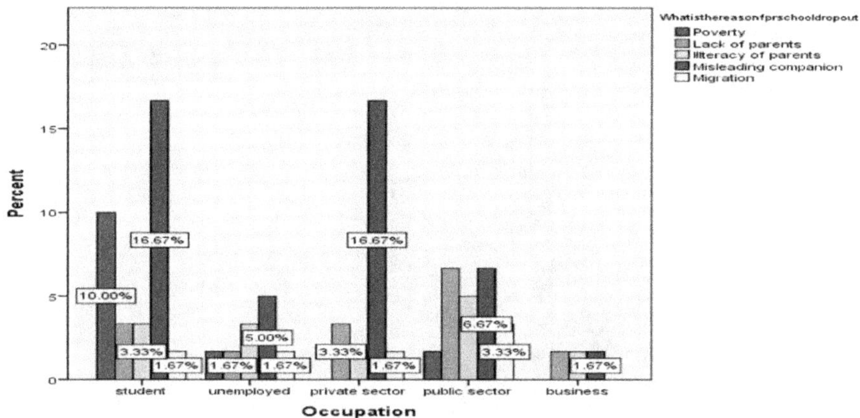

Legend : This figure deals with reasons for school dropouts with the independent variable occupation .

Result : Respondents from various occupations answered the question reasons for school dropouts, the student answered 10% on poverty,3.33% on lack of parents and illiteracy of parents, 16.67% on misleading companion and 1.67% on migration, the unemployed answered 1.67% on poverty , lack of parents,migration, 5% on misleading companion,the private sector covers 3.3% of respondents on lack of parents,1.67% on illiteracy of parents and migration and 16.67% on misleading companion, respondents on public sector answers 1.67% on poverty, 6.67% on lack of parents, misleading companion and illiteracy of parents and 3.3% on migration. The respondents on business profession answers 1.67% on poverty, illiteracy of parents,lack of parents.

Figure: 4

According to you, what is the reason for school dropouts.

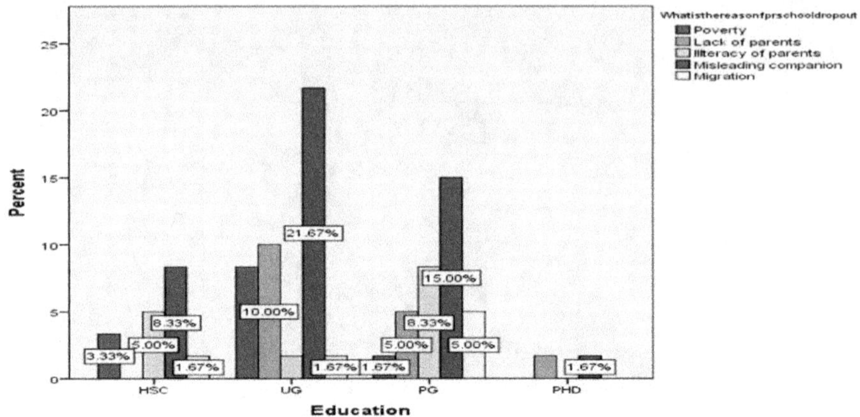

Legend : This figure deals with reasons for school dropouts with the independent variable Education .

Result : The respondents from different education qualifications answers the reason for school dropouts, respondents completed HSC answered 3.3% on poverty, 5% on illiteracy of parents, 8.3% on misleading companion ,1.67% on migration, respondents completed UG answered 10% on poverty and lack of parents, 1.67% on illiteracy of parents,21.67% on misleading companion, respondents completed PG answered 1.67% on poverty ,5% on lack of parents ,8.33% on illiteracy of parents,15% on misleading companion, 5% on migration, respondents completed PHD answered 1.67% on lack of parents and misleading companion.

Figure:5

On what percentage do you think school dropouts students are involved in crime?

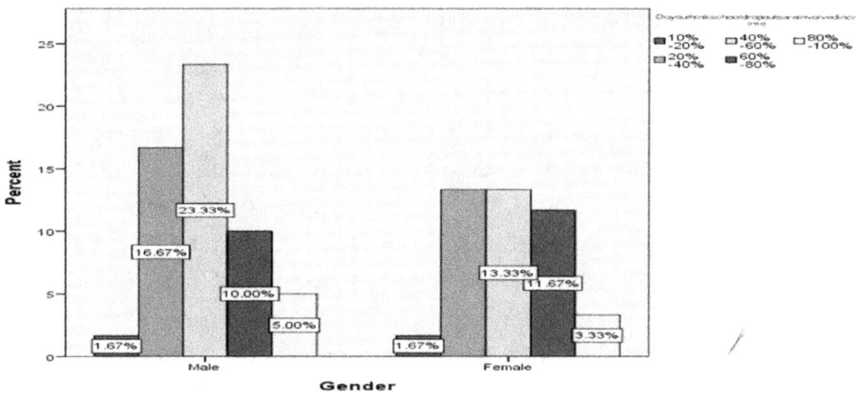

Legend :This figure deals with school dropouts students involved in crime, with the independent variable gender .

Result : Respondents composed of both male and female answer to the question school dropouts students involved in crime , the male respondents 1.67% on 10%-20% , 16.67% on 20%-40%,23.33% on 40%-60%,10% on 60%-80%,5% on 80%-100%,female respondents answered 1.67% on 10%-20%,13.33% on 20%-40% and 40%-60%,11.67% on 60%-80%, 3.3% on 80%-100%.

Figure :6

On what percentage do you think school dropouts are involved in crime?

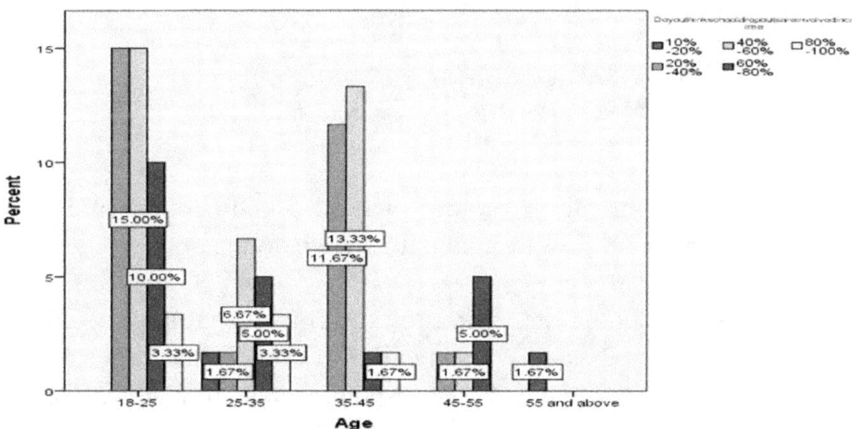

Legend :This figure deals with school dropouts students involved in crime, with the independent variable Age.

Result : Respondents from various age group answered to the question school dropouts students involved in crime , respondents belongs to 18-25 of age answer 15% of respondents on 20%-40% and 40%-60%,10% of respondents on 60%-80%,3.3% of respondents on 80%-100% and respondents belongs to age group 25 - 35 of age answer 1.67% on 10%-20% and 20%-40%, 6.67% of respondents on 40%-60%,5% of respondents on 60%-80% ,3.33% of respondents on 80%-100% , respondents belongs to age group 35-45 answers 11,67% of respondents on 20%-40%,13.33% of respondents on 40%-60%,1.67% of respondents on 60%-80% and 80%-100% , respondents from age group 45-55 , answers 1.67% on 20%-40% and 40%-60%,5% of respondents on 60%-80%, respondents belongs to 55 and above age answer 1.67% on 10%-20%.

Figure: 7

On what percentage do you think school dropouts are involved in crime?

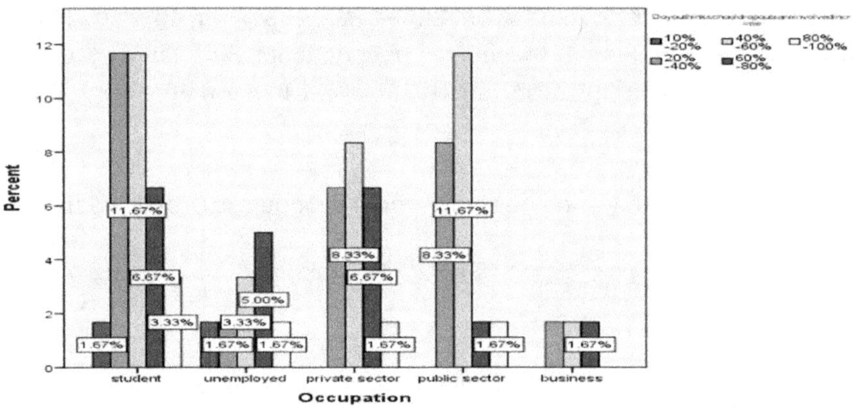

Legend : This figure deals with do you think school dropouts are involved in crime,with the independent variable occupation

Result: Respondents from various occupation answered to the question do you think school dropouts are involved in crime, and the respondents belongs to student answers 1.67% of respondents on 10%-20% , 11.67% of respondents on 20%-40% and 40%-60% ,6.67% of respondents on 60%-80% , 3.3% of respondents on 80%-100% , respondents belongs to unemployed answered 1.67% on 10%-40% ,3.33 % of respondents on 40%-60% ,5% of respondents on 60%-80% and 1.67% on 80-100% .the respondents belongs private sector answered 6.67% on 20%-40% and 60%-80% , 8.3% of respondents on 40%-60%, 1.67% of respondents on 80%-100%.respondents belongs to public sector answers 1.67% of respondents on 60%-80% and 80%-100% ,8.33% of respondents on 20%-40%,and 11.67% on 40%-60% .respondents belongs to business answers 1.67% on 20%-40% ,40%-60% and 60%-80%.

Figure :8

On what percentage do you think school dropouts are involved in crime?

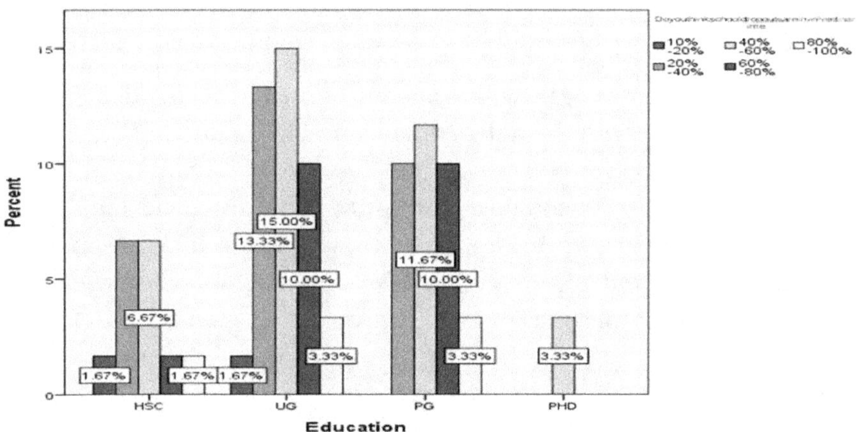

Legend : This figure deals with do you think school dropouts are involved in crime ,with the independent variable Education .

Result: Respondents from various qualifications answered to the question do you think school dropouts are involved in crime and the respondents completed to HSC answers 1.67% of respondents on 10%-20% , 6.67% on 20%-40% and 40%-60%, 1.67 % on 60%-80% and 80%-100%. respondents completed to UG answered 1.67% of respondents on 10%-20% , 13.3 % on 20%-40%, 15% on 40%-60% and 10% on 60%-80 and 3.33% on 80%-100% .The respondents completed PG answered 10% on 20%-40% and 60%-80% ,11. 67% of respondents on, 40%-60% and ,3.3% of respondents on 80%-100% , respondents completed PHD answers 3.33% On 40%-60%.

Figure: 9

Do you know someone who was a school dropout?

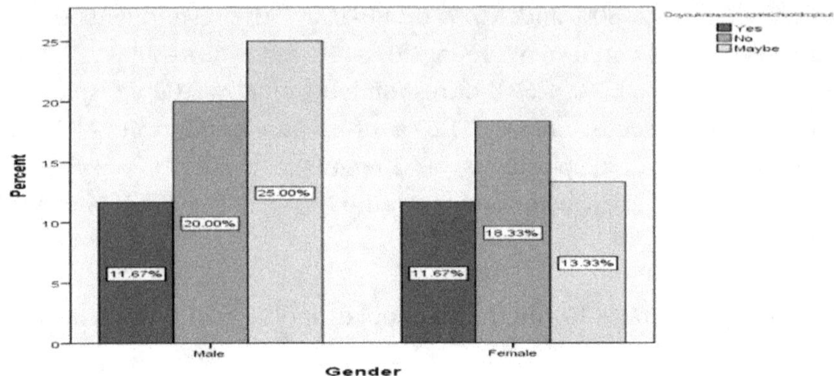

Legend : This figure deals with someone known by respondents who was school dropout,with the independent variable gender .

Result : Respondents composed of both male and female answered the question someone known by respondents who was school dropout, male respondents answered 11.67% on yes , 20% on no ,25% on maybe and the female respondents answered 11.67% on yes , 18.3% on no and 13.3% on maybe.

Figure :10

Do you know someone who was a school dropout?

Legend : This figure deals with someone known by respondents who was school dropout,with the independent variable Age.

Result :Respondents belonging to various age groups answered the question someone known by respondents who was a school dropout, respondents belongs to age 18-25 answers 11.67% on yes , 16.67% on no , 15% on maybe , respondents belongs to age group 25-35 answers 1.67% on yes, 6.67% on no , 10% on maybe , respondents belongs to age group 35-45 answers 6.67% on yes, 10% on no, 11.67% on maybe , respondents belongs to age group 45-55 answers 3.3% on yes and no , 1.67% on maybe , respondents belongs to age group 55 and above answers 1.67% on no .

Figure: 11

Do you know someone who was a school dropout?

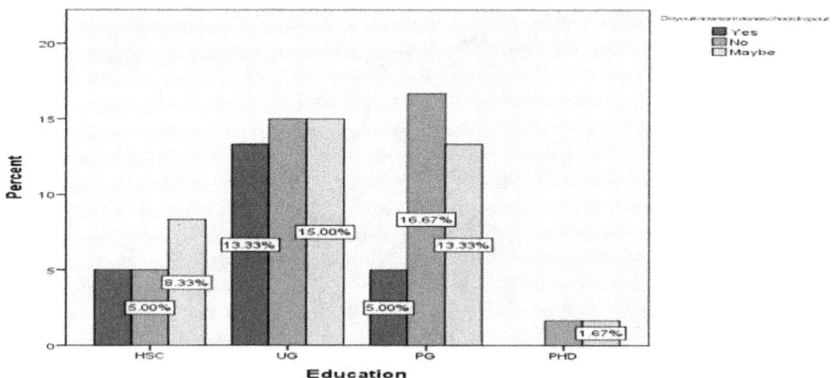

Legend : This figure deals with someone known by respondents who was school dropout,with the independent variable Education.

Result : Respondents belonging to various education qualifications answered to the question someone known by respondents who was a school dropout,

Respondents who completed HSC answers 5% on yes and no , 8.3% on maybe , respondents completed UG answers 13.3% on yes, 15% on no and maybe , respondents completed PG answers 5% on yes, 16.67% on no , 13.3% on maybe , respondents completed PHD , answers 1.67% on no and maybe .

Figure :12

Do you know someone who was a school dropout?

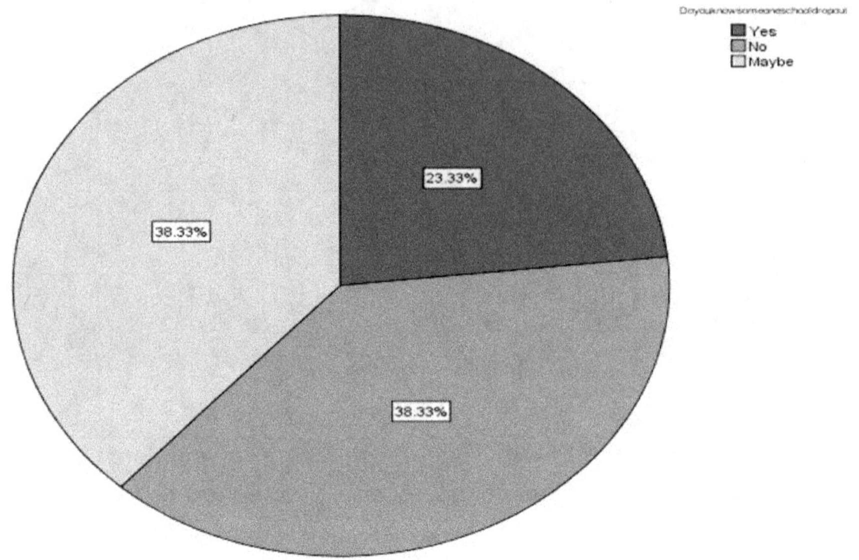

Legend : This figure deals with someone known by respondents who was school dropout,with the pie chart distribution.

Result : Respondents answered questions known by respondents who were school dropouts ,Respondents answered 23.33% on yes, 38.3% on no and 38.3% on maybe .

Figure :13

According to you, what is the reason for school dropouts.

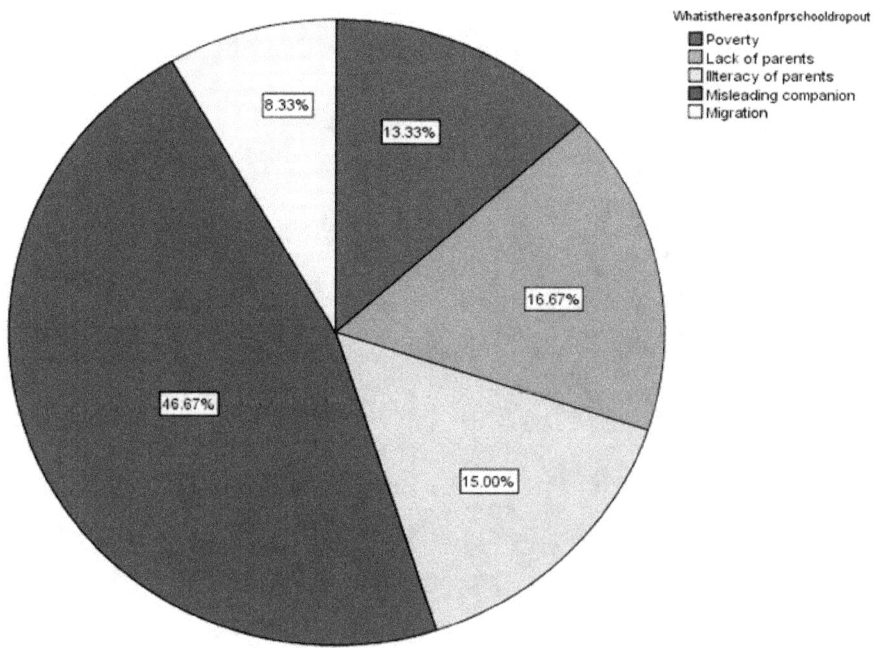

Legend : This figure deals with reasons for school dropouts with the pie chart distribution.

Result : Respondents answered the question reasons for school dropouts, 46.67% on misleading companions , 15% on illiteracy of parents , 16.67% on lack of parents ,13.3% on poverty, 8.3% on migration.

Figure : 14

On what percentage do you think school dropouts are involved in crime?

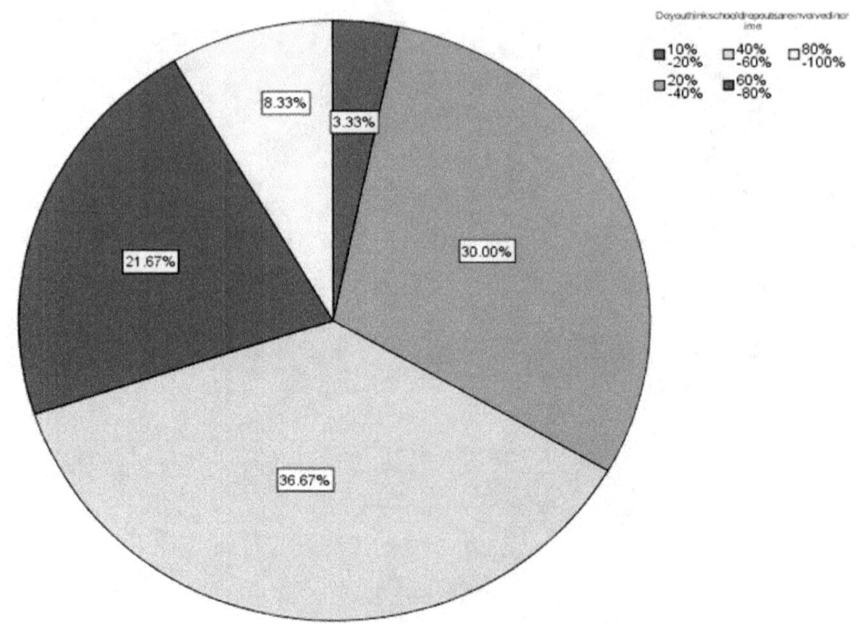

Legend : This figure deals with do you think school dropouts are involved in crime,with the pie chart distribution.

Result : Respondents answer to the question do you think school dropouts are involved in crime,3.3% of respondents on 10%-20%, 30 % of respondents on 20%-40%,36.67% of respondents on 40%-60%, 21.67% of respondents on 60%-80%, 8.3% of respondents on 80%-100%.

Discussion

Respondents from various age groups,gender , occupations and different qualifications answer the question reason for school dropout as 46.67% on misleading companions followed by 15% on illiteracy of parents , 16.67% on lack of parents ,13.3% on poverty, 8.3% on migration this shows majority of respondents opinionated misleading of friends in wrong way may leads a student to dropout their school , the migration falls lowest because respondents thought it has less contribution for dropout compare to illiteracy of parents that affect on school dropout and lack of parental care. (Figure 1,2,3,4 and 13)

Respondents from various age groups,gender , occupations and different qualifications answer their opinion on school dropouts are involved in crime, 21.67% of respondents on 60%-80%, 8.3% of respondents on 80%-100% this shows most of them answered many involved in crimes after dropout ,36.67% of respondents on 40%-60%,3.3% of respondents on 10%-20%, 30 % of respondents on 20%-40% this shows many also thought they may not involve in crime, this shows the respondents are neutral not all dropout students involved in crime.(Figure 5,6,7,8 and 14)

Respondents from various age groups,gender , occupations and different qualifications answer the question respondents know anyone who is school dropout answers 23.33% on yes, 38.3% on no and 38.3% on maybe , this shows many doesn't aware or know any dropout students, these maybe due to lack of social interaction or not many students are school dropout, however the reports stand the exist of School dropout, the 23% of respondents answers they know the school dropout students . (Figure 9,10,11,12) .

Limitation

The Major limitation of the study is the sample frame. The sample frame Collected through online platforms like sending mail, sending links via WhatsApp is the limitation of the study, the real field experience is missed out due to corona pandemic. There is no direct interaction with respondents yet another drawback of the research.Collection of data via online platforms is limiting the researcher to collect data from the field.

Conclusion

The school dropout is withdrawn from school , the education is the basic requirement that increase once income , the RTE act 2010 which enhance the enrolment, the main objective is to study the problems of students after dropout , to study the opportunities after dropout and to analyse their economic conditions and study factors leads to school dropout and the findings includes the reason for dropout highest respondents on misleading companion and lack of parental care ,the dropout students involved in crime many answers neutral this shows not all dropout involves in criminal activities,the need of better implementation of schemes and to create awareness about important of education and technology world education is much needed to sustain .

CHAPTER NINE

AN ANALYSIS ON THE EVOLUTION OF SURROGACY BILLS WITH SPECIAL REFERENCE TO 2019 AND 2020 BILL

Author: Chithra V, IV year of B.Com., LL.B(HONS) from School of Excellence in Law (The Tamilnadu Dr. Ambedkar Law University), Chennai.

Co-author: Mithra R, IV year of B.A.,LL.B(HONS) from School of Excellence in Law (The Tamilnadu Dr. Ambedkar Law University), Chennai.

Co-author: Krithika R, IV year of B.A.,LL.B(HONS) from School of Excellence in Law (The Tamilnadu Dr. Ambedkar Law University), Chennai.

ABSTRACT

With the development of science and technology in the field of reproduction, the creation of children now happens in many ways, one of which is surrogacy. In recent years, many children have been born through surrogacy. Women who accepted to be surrogate mothers benefited from it since it guaranteed their livelihood. On the other hand, the cost of surrogacy procedures in India was relatively cheaper when compared to other countries. Because of this, many foreigners came to rent surrogates and exploit poor women. This emphasised the need for proper laws to regulate the process of surrogacy in India. Only in the year 2016 was a bill drafted to regulate surrogacy procedures. Though it was drafted in the year 2016, it underwent many changes and finally became an act in the year 2021, i.e., the Surrogacy (Regulation) Act, 2021. This article attempts to discuss the evolution of surrogacy bills in India, analyse the 2019 and 2020 bills, and make suggestions as to how future laws on this subject should be made.

Keywords: technology, reproduction, surrogacy, surrogates.

INTRODUCTION

"There is such a special sweetness in being able to participate in creation." - Pamela S. Nadav[1] The term "surrogacy" is derived from the Latin word "surrogatus," which means a substitute or otherwise a person acting upon another. Black's Law Dictionary states surrogacy as "the process of carrying and delivering a child for another person."[2]The New Encyclopedia Britannica defines surrogacy as a practise in which a woman bears a child for a couple unable to produce children in the usual way.[3]

Surrogacy is a form of reproduction in which a woman consents to carry a baby for some other intending couple who cannot give birth naturally. The history of surrogacy goes back to 1978, when India's first IVF baby, Kanupriya, was born. India became the hub of surrogacy when it was legalised in 2002. There are two types of surrogacy practices: traditional and gestational. Traditional surrogacy is a process in which the surrogate mother will be the egg donor and the indenting father or other willing male will be the sperm donor for the creation of the child. Here, the surrogate mother will have a biological relationship with the child. In gestational surrogacy, the indenting mother or other willing female will be the egg donor, and the indenting father or other willing male will be the sperm donor for the creation of the child. Here, the surrogate mother will not have any biological relationship with the child.

The two types of surrogacy arrangements are:

• Commercial surrogacy
• Altruistic surrogacy

Commercial surrogacy is a method in which the surrogate mother will be carrying the child and will hand it over to the intending couple. For this process, she will be given monetary compensation beyond the medical expenses and the insurance coverage provided. It was made legal in 2002. However, ART Bill 2013 and subsequent surrogacy bills (2016, 2019, 2020) prohibit commercial surrogacy.

Altruistic surrogacy is a method in which the surrogate mother will be carrying the child and will hand it over to the intending couple. For this process, she will be given monetary compensation only for the medical expenses and the insurance coverage provided. Currently, this type of surrogacy is being practised in India.

EVOLUTION OF SURROGACY BILLS IN INDIA

2002: Commercial surrogacy was legalized. This was a boon for some surrogate mothers as it helped them to develop economically, it was also a bane for some surrogate mothers who were exploited for commercial purposes by the surrogate industries 2005: The Indian Council for Medical Research drafted some guidelines for surrogacy.

Procedures. As it didn't have any legal backing, it remained ineffective.

2008—In the landmark case Baby Manji Yamada v. Union of India (2007),

A Japanese couple, Dr. Yuki Yamada and Dr. Ifumuki, opted for a surrogate mother in India. A month before the baby was about to be born, the couple decided to part ways. The Mrs. Ifumuki was not ready to accept the child. As Yuki's visa expired, he had to flee to Japan. Yuki's mother came to India and took care of the newborn. A birth certificate is mandatory to apply for visa, so Yuki intended to apply her birth certificate for the child. But in this case, the child had three mothers (the intended mother, the egg, and donor, the surrogate). The question was about the legal mother of the child. Here, the court held that it is the Commission for the Protection of Child Rights Act, 2005 [4]. which has the power to look and decide the case. This raised a need for proper laws.

Relating to surrogacy procedures. This case led to the drafting of Assisted Reproductive Technologies Bill 2008, however, did not reach the Parliament bench. It was the first bill to deal with matters relating to surrogacy. 2010: The Assisted Reproductive Technology Bill, 2010, which specifically spoke about the

Rights and obligations of surrogate mothers and improvement of clinical trials

drafted on the recommendation made by the 228th report of the Law Commission.

According to this bill, a surrogate mother can give birth via surrogacy only five times in her lifetime, in addition to her own children. This bill requires informed consent from the parties who wish to opt for surrogacy.

2013: This bill prohibits surrogacy by foreigners, live-in partners, homosexuals, widows, and unmarried, parents who already have a child. According to this bill, a surrogate

A mother can give birth via surrogacy only three times in her lifetime, in addition to her own children. This bill requires written consent from the parties who wish to opt for surrogacy. A surrogate mother can make use of the insurance schemes (This is completely optional, and the surrogate child can also avail of this insurance scheme.) 2016—This was the first bill that was drafted by parliament to specifically deal with surrogacy. It attempted to define the term "surrogacy." It allowed only altruistic surrogacy and prohibited commercial surrogacy. Only one Indian couple who had been married for five years can opt for surrogacy (at least one must be infertile). The Women who wish to be a surrogate must be married and have a child of their own. It punishes a person who approaches any doctor or surrogacy clinics for commercial surrogacy. 2019 and 2020 Two major bills were introduced in 2019 and 2020 that regulated surrogacy procedures in India.The 2019 bill was rejected, and later in 2020. Another bill was introduced by Rajya Sabha and got its presidential assent on 25th December 2021.

Surrogacy Bill 2019

The bill was introduced by Dr. HarshaVardhan on July 15, 2019 and passed by the Lok Sabha on August 5. However, it did not get approval from the Rajya Sabha.

<u>**Key Features Of The 2019 Bill**</u>

Why is only altruistic surrogacy allowed?

Commercial surrogacy is more or less like a business, where the surrogate mothers are exploited by the surrogate agencies, who do it for the sake of money. After the introduction of commercial surrogacy, India became a big hub for other nations as the cost of surrogacy was comparatively less in India. This was the main reason for the ban on commercial surrogacy, as it leads to the exploitation of poor women. On the other hand, altruistic surrogacy doesn't involve money except for the medical expenses and the insurance coverage. This is the reason for permitting altruistic surrogacy in India.

Who can opt for surrogacy?

The 2019 bill set forth the following criteria for couples who wish to opt for surrogacy:

- The couples must be Indian citizens.
- At least one of them must be infertile.
- Age limit: males 26–55 years; females 25–50 years.
- 5 years of marriage life.
- no biological, adopted, or surrogate child.

Exception: a child with a mental or physical disability and a life-threatening disorder.

What are the essential criteria for surrogacy?

- The indenting couple must possess a certificate of essentiality.
- must possess a certificate of infertility.
- order by the court to take care of the child.
- 16 months of insurance coverage, which includes postpartum delivery difficulties.

Who can be a surrogate mother?

- Age limit: 25–35 years.
- She is married and must have a child of her own.
- must be a close relative of the intending couple.
- can be a surrogate mother only once in her lifetime.
- Written and informed consent from the surrogate mother (The surrogate has the option to withdraw her consent before the implantation of the embryo.)
- must possess a certificate of mental and physical fitness.

What does the bill say about surrogacy clinics?

- Only registered surrogacy clinics can opt for surrogacy procedures.
- An application for registration should be presented to the appropriate authority.
- This bill prohibits surrogacy clinics from permitting commercial surrogacy.
- not to conduct sex selection or determination procedures.
- not to advertise.

<u>What is the need for setting up surrogacy boards?</u>

The National Surrogacy Board
Quorum

- Minister of Health and Family Welfare (head)
- Secretary of the department
- 3 women members of the parliament
- 3 members, each from the ministry of women and child development, the ministry of law and justice, and the ministry of home affairs.

Functions

- aiding the government with regards to policy
- review and keep a track on the implementation of the law.
- listing the code of conduct and overseeing the state surrogacy boards.

State Surrogacy Board
Functions

- Evaluating appropriate authorities in the state
- reporting to both the government and the Central Surrogacy Board.

What constitutes offences and punishments for those according to this bill?

The offences mentioned in this bill are:

- Performing or advertising commercial surrogacy
- Overutilization of the surrogate mother
- Undertaking sex selection
- Trading of human embryos and gametes
- Neglecting the Newborn

All the above-mentioned offences attract imprisonment up to 10 years and a fine up to 10 lakh rupees. These offences are not bailable.

SURROGACY BILL 2020

After the select committee's recommendation, changes were made to the 2019 bill, which was passed by the Rajya Sabha on December 8, 2021. Further, it was sent to the Lok Sabha for approval. This bill got its approval from the Lok Sabha.

Amendements made to the 2019 Bill (2020 Bill)

- Any willing woman can opt for surrogacy. (includes widows and divorcees)
- A surrogate mother can avail of insurance coverage for 36 months, including postpartum difficulties.
- Not only infertility but also any other medical conditions that necessitate gestational surrogacy can also be grounds for surrogacy.
- The intended mother's minimum age limit was reduced from 25 to 23 years.
- makes registration of surrogacy clinics mandatory.

This bill received the assent of the President on December 25, 2021, and became the Surrogacy (Regulation) Act, 2021.

<u>Analyses of the 2019 and 2020 bills</u>

Violation of the Indian Constitutional Provisions

Article 14 guarantees equality before the law.

According to this Article, "The State shall not deny to any person equality before the law or the equal protection of the laws within the territory of India." [5]

Both the 2019 and 2020 bills exclude homosexuals, live-in partners, divorced people, and the unmarried. This apparently violates Article 14, as the 2019 and 2020 bills include only heterosexual couples. It is required that there be a relationship between the classification and the purpose of the legislation. But the classification made in this bill has nothing to do with the purpose of the bill. Even after the recognition of the LGBTQ community by the courts and society, the passing of such bills is a complete injustice.

In the Navtej Singh Johar v. Union of India [6] case, it was held that any legislation that discriminates against any individual based on their sexual orientation violates Article 14. Both the bills are drafted against the decision in this case.

Article 21[7] states that "No person shall be deprived of his life or personal liberty except according to a procedure established by law."

Rights to livelihood, privacy, and reproductive autonomy come under the ambit of Article 21.

Right to livelihood: Since these bills prohibit commercial surrogacy, women who act as surrogate mothers to fulfil their daily needs will be affected.

Right to privacy: Opting for surrogacy is a personal choice for an individual. A state cannot interfere in people's personal choices by introducing such bills. The same was held in Puttaswamy's case. In K.S. Puttaswamy v. Union of India [8], the Supreme Court recognised the right to privacy as a fundamental right for the first time in India.

Right to reproductive autonomy: Every woman has her own choice of reproduction. Since these bills impose restrictions on that, it violates the right to reproductive autonomy.

The following are some of the international provisions that are being violated:

UDHR (Universal Declaration of Human Rights) [9]

Article 12 (Right to Privacy)

Article 16 (Right to marry and start a family)

ICCPR (International Covenant on Civil and Political Rights) [10]

Article 17 (Right to Privacy)

ICESCR (International Covenant on Economic, Social, and Cultural Rights) [11]

Article 10 (Right to Parenthood)

<u>CONCLUSION</u>

The Surrogacy (Regulation) Act 2021 has both pros and cons. Though it protects women from being overexploited, it also takes away some of their rights. This Act should be amended in such a way that it does not discriminate against anyone on the basis of sexual orientation. Since the surrogate mothers dedicate nearly a year for the reproduction, reasonable monetary compensation beyond the medical expenses and insurance coverage can be provided to them. If any future laws are made on this subject, they must include homosexuals, live-in partners, divorced people, and the unmarried.

"Biology is the least of what makes someone a mother"—Oprah Winfrey [12]

CHAPTER TEN

THE PSYCHOLOGY OF JUDICIAL SENTENCING

Author: Anshika Srivastava, I year of B.A.,LL.B.(Hons.) from Rajiv Gandhi National University of Law, Patiala

Judges are powerful leaders. We are all impacted by their actions, whether directly or indirectly.However, the majority of us have rarely considered how judges handle the peculiar task ofconverting their dislike of offenders into years, pounds, or hours of punishment. The psychologyof judicial sentencing raises several unanswered problems, such as why no judge has everimposed a five-month term of imprisonment. Why don't judges raise concerns about remissionand parole, which can lower sentences by as much as two-thirds? Why, in the face of all theevidence to the contrary, do they still hold such a strong belief in thedistinctive effects of theirsentences? We will discuss the psychology of judgment errors in this blog, as well as the beliefthat judges accurately reflect the opinion of the people, the psychology of presentingexplanations, and the challenging task of translating a perception of an offence and offendersinto the "correct punishment".

If hundreds of criminal court judges were asked what aspect of their work they found the mostchallenging, the overwhelming majority would very definitely respond, "Sentencing".No otherjudicial duty leaves the judge more isolated, and no other decision he makes has more potentialfor good or bad than deciding how society will handle its violators.[i]The psychology and math ofprison terms are among the special themes, along with mitigation and sentencing discrepancy.The process of court sentencing involves human judgment and decision-making, with all of itsdrawbacks and restrictions. Explaining this procedure and its results requires a close look at howjudges compile, analyse, and use information regarding criminals.[ii]

The necessity for regulation of the criminal justice system across every nation is urgent given theworrisome rise in crime rates in today's world. Today, crime and punishment make up a highlyimportant and delicate component of society; they can no longer be controlled by traditionsandestablished precedents. It is necessary to implement a fixed regime and to minimize thesubjective component as much as feasible. However, it cannot be forgotten that the accused maynot receive any specific sanctions since they are too harsh and unaware of their rights. Beforecreating a punishment strategy, it is necessary to strike an equilibrium between the interests ofthe two victims. The criminal conviction and the society will both influence the type ofpunishment administered. Some communities only care about the victim, but others care moreabout rehabilitating the offender than about punishing them. The sentencing guidelines show the society's level of judgment and justification for a certain offence. A judge will determine theappropriate sentence at the sentencing stage of a criminal proceeding when a criminal defendantis found guilty or enters a plea of guilt. Depending on the offence and the prisoner, the court mayin some cases be able to increase or decrease a sentence. Fines, imprisonment, probation, asuspended sentence, community work, restitution, and engagement in rehabilitation programs areall possible punishments.[iii]

Although judges do have the last say in penalties, they are limited in what they canaccomplishby the statutes and sentencing guidelines that are in place in each state. Since the late 1970s,judicial discretion has been constrained by the creation of sentencing laws and other methods forstructuring the sentence decision. Others argue that additional measures, such as mandatoryminimum sentencing restrictions, are necessary to further restrict judicial discretion, while someclaim that these arrangements excessively restrict a judge's capacity to take all pertinent factorsinto account before rendering a decision.[iv]It is important to recognize that the focus on judicialsentencing is a result of a major shift in sentencing theories. In the 1970s, a regime of "indeterminate punishment" was replaced by one based on the principle of "fair deserts". Twokey elements were integrated with indeterminate sentencing. First, with the exception oflegislatively mandated maximums and (less frequently) minimums, judicial authority insentencing was broad and usually uncontrolled. Second, the actual amount of time that offendersspent in custody was determined by the release decisions made by state parole boards, whichwere appointed by the governor, and who were matched with the judicial decisions concerningsentence duration.

Although Minnesota's sentencing guidelines accept the concept of just deserts, "attorneys as wellas trial judges remain strongly connected to offender-based crime control punishment goals" andthe application of judicial discretion has progressively grown. Some of the movement's mostprominent proponents claimed that one of the movement's main objectives was to improvejudicial discretion by restricting the "back end" jurisdiction of parole boards. They also point outthe particular accountability that judges have for their sentence judgments.[v]

Since each offender is now seen as an individual, the sentencing judge asks the offender why hedid the crime and what the likelihood is that he may repeat it again. The judge's main goal is totreat rather than punish. Numerous new issues have arisen as a result of the emphasis placed ontreating the individual. Judges must consider an overwhelming number of factors in order todetermine the appropriate course of action for specific inmates. I think that every sentence's mainobjective should be to deter future criminality.[vi]There isn't much that can be done to undo theharm done in the past, and a sentence would succeed in its goal if it respects the rule of law,deters those who might be tempted to conduct similar crimes, and results in the offender'srehabilitation so that he won't break the law again. The judge must be as informed as possibleabout the prisoner who is in front of him. He should understand how the convict is likely torespond to incarceration or probation as well as the expected implications of penalties onindividuals who could conduct similar offences. He is well aware that, in many circumstances, ajail sentence not only shortens the lifespan of the inmate but also taints the lives of uninvolvedfamily members. Every judge is keenly aware of the potential impact fatherlessness may have ona prisoner's son after five years.

However, society must be safeguarded, a criminal activity must be discouraged, violentoffenders must be isolated, and convicts must be reformatted. The optimal sentence to achievethese goals must be chosen by someone. The judge is responsible for this responsibility in federalcourts, although the person who is convicted would face the same issues regardless of his position.

CHAPTER ELEVEN

PRACTICALITIES ASSOCIATED WITH ADMISSIBILITY OF ELECTRONIC EVIDENCE

Author: Falguni Vivek Suryawanshi, IV year of B.A.,LL.B.(Hons.) from Maharashtra National Law University, Mumbai

Co-author: Dhanashree Balasaheb Kolte, IV year of B.A.,LL.B.(Hons.) from Maharashtra National Law University, Mumbai

INTRODUCTION

The advent of Information and Communication Technology has an enormous impact on various arenas like Trade & Commerce, thereby, impacting the way people communicate and transact business. Hence, with the increase in the use of cyberspace in daily activities, electronic evidences play a vital role in dispute resolution. Therefore, it is inevitable that the rules of admissibility should reflect the technological changes. Owing to the rapid technological changes, various nations are enacting new legislations and streamlining the existing laws accordingly. Similarly, India has enacted the Information Technology Act, 2000 (ITA) to primarily encourage and legitimize e-business and through the same Act, also amended its Indian Evidence Act, 1872 (IEA) especially on the issue of recognition, admissibility and appreciation of electronic evidence.

However, electronic evidence as opposed to traditional rules of authenticating documentary evidence is difficult to implement. Electronic evidence being easy to manipulate, create, copy or destroyed, may not have a strong evidentiary value as physical evidence. The evidence has to be proved 'beyond a reasonable doubt' and the admissibility of electronic evidence owing to the multiple risks is questionable. The article seeks to critically examine the rules of electronic admissibility using various statutes and judicial pronouncements. It purports to pinpoint the practical problems associated with the current settled position by highlighting both, legal and technical lacunas.

Evidence also includes electronic evidence under Indian Evidence Act which is any ESI (Electronic Stored Information) generated by some mechanical or electronic processes which can be used as evidence during a case before the court. Electronic evidence can be documents, E-mails, CDs or DVDs, or other files which are stores electronically.[i] Addition, it includes records which are stored by Internet or network service providers.

Section 65B of the Indian Evidence Act gives the procedure for justification of any documentary evidence by the way of an electronic record. It states that any information which is contained in an electronic record i.e., engrave on a paper, stored, recorded or copied in any optical or magnetic media which is produced by a computer shall be considered as a document if it fulfills the condition laid down under section 65B (2) to 65B (5).[ii] These conditions should be taken into consideration while proving the admissibility of anyelectronic evidence.

1. Audio & Video Recorded Conversations

It is a well settled legal proposition that the tape recorded conversation can be used as a primary and direct evidence. Therefore, tape records of speeches,[iii]audio/video cassettes,[iv]compact discs[v]are 'documents' under Section 3 of Indian Evidence Act, 1872. They are as similar as photographs and therefore are admissible. However, the Courts have laid parameters in order to admit such conversations. The tape recorded conversations can be used to corroborate evidence given by the witness, contradict the evidence, test the veracity of the witness, or impeach the impartiality. It is not only confined to corroboration or contradiction but also extends to be used as substantive evidence.[vi]

In R.M. Malkaniv. State of Maharashtra,[vii]the Supreme Court has held that the tape recorded conversation is admissible and is a relevant fact provided that the conversation is relevant to the matters in issue, secondly, there is identification of the voice: and, thirdly, the accuracy of the tape recorded conversation is proved by eliminating the possibility of erasing the tape record.

In Ram Singh and Ors. v. Ram Singh,[viii]the Court laid down the conditions for admissibility of tape recorded conversations provided that the following conditions are fulfilled-

The voice must be duly identified. Where the voice has been denied by the maker it will require very strict proof to determine whether or not it was really the voice of the speaker.

a) The maker has to prove the record by satisfactory evidence- direct or circumstantial.

b) The maker has to rule out all the possibility of tampering

c) The statement must be relevant according to Indian Evidence Act.

d) The recorded cassette must be carefully sealed and kept in safe and official custody.

e) The voice should be clear and not distorted by other sounds or disturbances.

The Court has relied upon tape recorded reproductions in Ziyauddin Burhanuddin Bukhariv. Brijmohan Ramdass Mehra and Ors.[ix]The Court clearly laid out that the tape recorded speeches if not tampered with, were the best form of evidence available with respect to the statements recorded thereto. However, the Court had laid down three grounds for considering tape records to be reliable and authentic. Firstly, the tape records should be prepared and preserved safely by an independent authority. Secondly, the transcripts from the tape records, shown to have been duly prepared under independent supervision and control, very soon afterwards, made subsequent tempering with the cassettes easy to detect; and, thirdly, the police had should not use it for the purpose of laying any trap to procure evidence.

In Yusufalli Esmail Nagreev. The State of Maharashtra,[x]the Court pondered on the fact that tape recording have the ability to erase and re-use the recording medium. Therefore, the evidence must be received with caution. The time, place and accuracy of the recordings have to be proved by the competent witness and the voices must be properly identified. The Court must be satisfied beyond reasonable doubt that the record has not been tampered with.

2. WhatsApp conversations

Section65A and 65B of Indian Evidence Act laysdown the conditions that are required to be met in the case of producing WhatsApp evidences in court. The party which is producing WhatsApp evidence has to provide a certificate from a Forensic Laboratory stating the details of the electronic records in order for Courts to admit the electronic records as evidence. WhatsApp conversationsare admissible in the Court of Law as evidence provided that the conditions enlisted in Section65A and 65B.

In Ambala Sarabhai Enterprise v. Ks InfraspaceLlp Limited,[xi]The Supreme Court made areference of WhatsApp messages produced as evidence. The Court held that the WhatsApp messages being virtual verbal communications are matters of evidence with regard to their meaning and its contents to be proved during trial by evidence-in-chief and cross examination. However, there are differing opinions by various courts on the issue whether certification under Section 65B is mandatory for WhatsApp messages to be of any evidentiary value.

Forinstance, In Rakesh Kumar Singla v. Union of India[xii] (Punjab and Haryana High Court) the learned council placed reliance on WhatsApp messages that could implicate the petitioner for granting bail. However, on asking of the Court, the certificate under Section 65B of the Indian Evidence Act isavailable for authentication of messages couldn't be produced.

In this case, the Supreme Court placed reliance on Arjun Panditrao Khotkar v. Kailash Kushanrao Gorantyal,[xiii]where in it mandated the certification of Section 65B of Indian Evidence Act if reliance is placed upon electronic record. In case, no certificate is provided then the said message is of no evidentiary value.

Whereas, in Chirag Dipakbhai Sulekha v. State of Gujarat,[xiv]the Gujrat High Court granted bail placing reliance on WhatsApp messages between the two parties in question concluding that they know each other very well and that there a relationship between them. Further,inKaranChhabraand Ors. v. State of Haryana[xv]where three students of Jindal Global University were accused ofgangrapingandblackmailingtheirjunior,thecourtdirectlyadmittedWhats App chats as evidence and stated that these messages have played a concomitant role in corroborating the intention andadducingto thecommission of the offence.

3. Emails

There are differing opinions with regards to admissibility of email as evidence. In Kundan Singhv. The State,[xvi]the Delhi High Court explained that a computer output is treated as evidence when the provision under section 65B of the Indian Evidence Act is fulfilled. Such evidence is admissible in the Court and the onus of proving its originality lies in the person who sought to produce it as evidence. Here certificate under section

65B is mandatory.

The High Court of Calcutta in Abdul RahamanKunji v. The State of West Bengal,[xvii]stated that emails downloaded and printed from an individual's email record and proved under section 65B with respect to section 88A of Indian Evidence Act is admissible in the Court as electronic evidence.

However, in Mr. S. Karunakaran v. Ms. Srileka,[xviii]emails were presented to prove the relationship between the parties in question. The Madras High Court stated that telegraphic materials cannot be received as evidence. Mere filing of such email, it cannot be said that those emails have been proved as per law and that sending of electronic messages and emails has to be proved. The Court cannot presume that it was the plaintiff that has sent such emails. As long as proof as to who has sent such email is established, it is highly difficult to presume that only the plaintiff has sent such email, the emails cannot be given much importance, without its proof.

4. Hard-disc and Photographs

On whether hard disc can be used as documentary evidence, the Delhi High Court in Dharambirv. Central Bureau of Investigation[xix]observed that as long as the hard disc is subjected to no change, it is a mere storage device. As soon as the blank hard disc is written upon, it becomes an electronic record. Even if the hard disc is restored to its original form of a blank hard disc by erasing what was recorded on it, it would still retain information which indicates that some text or file in any form was recorded on it and was subsequently removed.

Photographs - In another case of PuneetPrakash v. Suresh Kumar Singhal&Anr,[xx]the Court states that when photographs are taken digitally and the person who took the photographs and himself has deposed in the Court, his mere statement that he got photograph developed himself is sufficient and satisfy the requirements of Section 65B of the Evidence Act. A digital photograph which is proved constitutes electronic evidence, which is admissible.

PRACTICAL ISSUES

1. Accuracy of Electronic Evidence

Identification of any said electronic record is of primary concern for the Courts to admit such record as evidence. A certificate under section 65B is mandatory for the admissibility of the electronic evidence. On top of that, Court seeks the creator of the record in question to testify on who the author of the said electronic record is. The reliability of the documentation of the computer data is questioned along with the performance of the computer. If the documentation is tampered with, after the document has been created. For example, if a photograph is photo-shopped, altered, changed, or hacked during the process.

2. Primary evidence or Secondary Evidence

There is a blurred boundary between primary and secondary evidence when it comes to electronic evidences. As the data derived is computer-generated, it is difficult to present its physical form in the Court. As a consequence, if the word document is the original, a printout of the same might be considered as secondary evidence. Producing a word document in courtwithout the use ofprintoutsor CDs is verydifficult.

3. Time Consuming

The whole process of issuing a certificate (from Forensic Labs) under section 65B of Evidence Act is quite time consuming and it can take months to authenticate an electronic device. Also, there lacks such Forensic labs for authentication process of electronic evidence. Further, testimony ofnumerouspeopleis timeconsuming.

4. Expert Testimony

Expert testimony can be used in court only if it was provided by an expert rather than a layman. A layperson's testimony is not admissiblein court.

5. WhatsApp Calls

In normal calls, through CDR's and SDR's, one can track the authentic call records and relevantinformation which is admissible in Court. But if a WhatsApp call is made, there's no way suchcallscould be traced as thedata onWhatsApp is encrypted.

6. Lack of Training and Expertise

Poor knowledge of electronic and forensic techniques is affecting the quality of police probes and impacting the conviction rate, hence, hindering the process of justice. Since virtual world isdifferent and the investigator cannot apply traditional evidence procedures as this evidence is nottangible and perceptible.

7. Standard Operating Process/ Guidelines for Storing, Collection and Acquisition

There are no set guidelines as to on what basis should an electronic evidence be admissible in the court. The judges have a discretionary power over this decision. Hence, what is admissible for one judge might not be the same for another. Also, there are no proper guidelines for collection andacquisition of the evidence. Finally, if the digital evidence is made inadmissible in court due to problems in handling it appropriately. The investigation team and forensic labs have different sets of guidelines making it inconsistent especiallywhen cyber spacehas no territorialboundaries.

8. Manipulation of the evidence

As the process of certification and preservation of the evidence being time consuming, there is a high risk of manipulation of electronic evidence through hacking, etc. For instance, if an electronic device is to be sent in another city for authentication process and such device comes in contactwith any magnetic substance present around it, there is a chance that the data might be hampereddueto themagneticwaves.

9. Ambiguityinjudgments

There is an ambiguity in the certification under section 65B of the Indian Evidence Act. Forinstance, some of the Courts have admitted WhatsApp conversations without the certificationrequired under section 65B of Evidence Act.

<u>CONCLUSION</u>

The process of recording electronic documentation has both ethical and societal problems. Mobile phones contain all sorts of information about various aspects of our life. In recent years, the media has placed a larger focus on electronic data collecting. The most significant issue is whether to rely on such electronic information and the utilization of knowledge acquired from electronic devises and networks. Establishing a regulatory framework, addressing numerous legal concerns and considering future challenges are all required in this time and age.